THE
AMERICAN
WEST

A HISTORY SOURCEBOOK

THE AMERICAN WEST

NATIVE AMERICANS, PIONEERS AND SETTLERS

CHRISTINE HATT

PETER BEDRICK BOOKS

NEW YORK

Published by
Peter Bedrick Books
156 Fifth Avenue
New York, NY 10010

© 1998 Evans Brothers Limited

Library of Congress Cataloging–in–Publication Data

Hatt, Christine
    The American West : Native Americans, pioneers and settlers/
Christine Hatt.
        p. cm. – – History in writing
    Summary: Surveys the settling of the American West, using
excerpts from contemporary sources to highlight the original
Native American inhabitants, the arrival of fur traders, the Gold
Rush, Mormon migrations, the growth of cattle-ranching, and
more.
    ISBN 0–87226–290–1 (hc)
    1. West (U.S.) – – History – – Sources – – Juvenile literature.
2. West (U.S.) – – History – – Miscellanea – – Juvenile
literature. [1.West (U.S.) History.] I. Title. II. Series
F591.H287 1998
978 – – dc21   98–27698
                                                        CIP
                                                        AC

Design – Neil Sayer
Editorial – Kath Davies
Maps – Tim Smith
Consultant – Karen D. Harvey
Production – Jenny Mulvanny

Title page picture: Fort Laramie by Alfred Jacob Miller,1837

Artists of the American West

There are thousands of pictures of the American West. Some
artists became famous, others remain unknown. Many
pictures show the romantic dreams of the painters, rather than
the reality of life in the West. The American artists noted below
are famous for the accuracy of their observation as well as
their skill. Some of their pictures appear in this book.

George Catlin, 1796-1872

Catlin spent eight years in the West, between 1829 and
1837. He made about 500 paintings of Native American life,
which were exhibited in Europe and the USA between 1837
and 1845.

Alfred Jacob Miller, 1810-1874

In 1837 Miller travelled to the West with a hunting expedition.
His pictures are of scenery and the lives of hunters, fur
trappers and Native Americans.

Frederic Remington, 1861-1909

From 1888, Remington travelled in the West for health
reasons. He painted more than 2700 pictures of Native
Americans, soldiers, cowboys and horses. His work was
published in magazines such as Harper's Weekly.

ACKNOWLEDGEMENTS

For permission to reproduce copyright pictorial material, the author
and publishers gratefully acknowledge the following:
Cover (top right) and **page 17** (left) Beinecke Rare Book and
Manuscript Library, Yale University. **Cover** (bottom left and right), **title
page**, **page 6** (left), **7**, **8**, **9**, **10** (top and bottom), **12**, **13** (top), **14**,
15 (top), **17** (right), **18**, **19**, **20**, **22**, **23** (bottom left), **25**, **26** (top
left and bottom), **28**, **29**, **30**, **31**, **32**, **33**, **34** (top), **35** (left), **36**
(top), **37**, **38** (left), **39**, **40**, **42** (top), **43** (left), **44** (top left and
right), **45**, **46**, **47**, **48**, **51**, **53**, **54**, **55**, **56** (top), **57** Peter Newark's
Western Americana. **page 11** British Library. **page 13** (bottom)
Walter Rawlings/Robert Harding Picture Library. **page 6** (right) and
page 15 (centre) Kentucky State Historical Society/University of
London Library. **cover** (centre), **16**, **21**, **26** (top right), **42** (bottom),
56 (bottom) UPI/Corbis. **page 23** (top right), **34** (bottom), **36**
(bottom), **44** (bottom), **50** Corbis-Bettman. **page 35** (right) Fort
Collins Public Library. **page 38** (right) Courtesy, Colorado Historical
Society: **page 43** (right) Jim Petrillo/Mary Strickler's Quilt shop,
California. **page 52** Private Collection/Bridgeman Art Library. **page
58** (top) Bridgeman Art Library (bottom) Private Collection/Bridgeman
Art Library.

For permission to reproduce copyright material for the documents, the
author and publishers gratefully acknowledgge the following:
page 9 From Blackfoot Lodge Tales by George B. Grinnell. Published
by the University of Nebraska Press **page 11** British Library **page 13**
The Tlinglit from Nora Marks Dauenhauer and Richard Dauenhauer
Haa Shuka, Our Ancestors: Tlingit Oral Narratives (Seattle, 1987)
page 19 From The West of Alfred Jacob Miller, University of Oklahoma
Press 1968 **page 21** (bottom) From A People's History of the United
States by Howard Zinn. Reprinted by permission of Addison Wesley

Longman Ltd. **page 23 and 49** Excerpt from Voices of the American
Past: Documents in U.S. History, Volume 2 by Raymond Hyser and J.
Chris Arndt, copyright © 1994 by Harcourt Brace & Company,
reprinted by permission of the publisher. **page 25** (top) Jones, Mary
Ann Smith, Recollections of Mary A. Jones (BANC MSS C-D 5090),
The Bancroft Library, University of California, Berkeley **page 25, 45
and 51** From The Great West, A Treasury of Firsthand Accounts, edited
by Charles Neider. Copyright © 1958, 1986 by Charles Neider.
Used with the permission of Charles Neider. **page 27** (bottom)
Reproduced in Pioneer Children on the Journey West by Werner.
Copyright (c) 1996 by Westview Press. Reprinted by permission of
Westview Press. **page 29** (top) **and page 36** (top) From The West An
Illustrated History by Geoffrey C Ward. Published by Weidenfeld and
Nicolson. **page 7 and 31** This item is reproduced from HM 538,
diary of Catherine Haun by permission of The Huntington Library, San
Marino, California. **page 35** State Historical Society of Wisconsin.
page 36, 39 and 55 From Cowboy Culture by David Dary. Copyright
(c) 1981 by David Dary. Reprinted by permission of Alfred A Knopf
Inc. **page 41** (top) **and page 46** With kind permission of Wordsworth
Editions **page 43** With kind permission of the Nebraska State
Historical Society. **page 49** (top) Army and Navy Journal, 16 Feb,
1867. **page 53 and 59** Reprinted by permission of the Peters Fraser
and Dunlop Group Ltd. **page 59** Copyright © 1967, from The Gold
Rush Diary of Elisha Perkins, 11 July 1849, by Thomas D. Clark.
Reprinted with permission of The University Press of Kentucky. Whilst
every effort has been made to secure permission to use copyright
material, Evans Brothers apologise for any errors or omissions in the
above list and would be grateful for notification of any corrections to
be included in subsequent editions.

CONTENTS

LOOKING AT DOCUMENTS

The American West looks at the gradual arrival of non-Native Americans in the West. At the center of the story are the 19th-century migrations of European Americans, but other groups also made vital contributions to the history of the West. They include the Mexicans who imported their cattle-farming skills, the Chinese and Irish who built the transcontinental railroads, and the African Americans who fled there to escape discrimination.

The settler communities developed new ways of life in family homes, on cattle ranches, in religious settlements and wild frontier towns. This book looks at these lifestyles, and how they changed as the 19th century drew to a close. It also makes clear the terrible, lasting cost of Western settlement to the Native American peoples.

To bring this story to life, *The American West* uses a wide range of documents – diaries of overlanders and cowboys, newspaper articles, speeches made by Native American leaders and others. There are photographs of some of these. To make the documents easier to read, they are printed in modern type.

Think carefully about the documents. When were they written – when the West was unknown territory or when many people had settled there? Where were they written – from a distance, or in the region? Above all who wrote them? Pioneers making their way across the continent and Native Americans lamenting the loss of their homelands will have very different views. The answers to such questions will help you to decide how reliable each document may be. No single document can give a complete picture, but together, they show something of people's experience of the American West.

The extracts on these pages show how varied the documents are, and explain how and why some of them were written.

 Political and legal documents, such as the US Declaration of Independence, 1776, help to explain the historical background at the time when settlers were moving into the American West (see page 12).

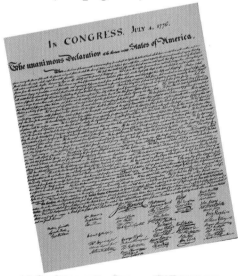

 Exciting accounts of explorers encouraged many people to set out for the West. In 1784, John Filson published the story of Daniel Boone, explorer of Kentucky (see page 15).

'Three days after, we were fired upon again, and had two men killed, and three wounded. Afterwards we proceeded on to Kentucke river without opposition; and on the first day of April began to erect the fort of Boonsborough at a **salt lick**, about sixty yards from the river, on the S. side. . .'

What does this mean? Some words and phrases in the document are difficult to understand. The captions explain the highlighted areas of text. You can find out what 'salt lick' means on page 15.

THE
DISCOVERY, SETTLEMENT
And present State of
K E N T U C K E:
A N D
An ESSAY towards the TOPOGRAPHY,
and NATURAL HISTORY of that im-
portant Country:
To which is added,
An A P P E N D I X,
C O N T A I N I N G,
I. The ADVENTURES of Col. *Daniel Boon*, one
of the first Settlers, comprehending every im-
portant Occurrence in the political History of
that Province.
II. The MINUTES of the *Piankashaw* coun-
cil, held at *Post St. Vincents, April* 15, 1784.
III. An ACCOUNT of the *Indian* Nations in-
habiting within the Limits of the Thirteen U-
nited States, their Manners and Customs, and
Reflections on their Origin.
IV. The STAGES and DISTANCES between
Philadelphia and the Falls of the *Ohio*; from
Pittsburg to *Pensacola* and several other Places.
—The Whole illustrated by a new and accu-
rate MAP of *Kentucke* and the Country ad-
joining, drawn from actual Surveys.
By J O H N F I L S O N.
Wilmington, Printed by JAMES ADAMS, 1784.

There are many accounts of how Native Americans helped early explorers in the West. The journals of Lewis and Clark (see page 17) record how a Shoshone woman helped on their expedition to find a route to the Pacific Ocean.

Life as a cowboy on a cattle trail was hard but enjoyable for many (see page 37). Clarence W. Gordon was an agricultural agent who listed preparations for a cattle drive.

Catherine Haun and her husband left Iowa for California, joining the Gold Rush of 1849 (see pages 30, 31).

'... Having bought the cattle ... he goes to some horse ranch and buys ... say 40 horses for each average drove of 2,300 to 2,500 cattle. He also engages about a dozen cowboys for each such drove ... Having made these engagements, and purchased a camp wagon ... he started out on the trail....'

You can find out what all these words mean on page 21.

As more settlers moved into the West, the Native American peoples were driven off their lands into reservations. Leaders such as Tecumseh, of the Shawnee people, tried to unite their people and to negotiate with the American government for just treatment. Tecumseh's words were recorded (see pages 20, 21).

'... The **being within**, communing with past ages, tells me that ... until lately, there was no white man on this continent. ... all belonged to **red men**, ... placed on it by the **Great Spirit** ... Once a happy race. Since made miserable by the white people, who are never contented but always encroaching. The way ... to stop this evil, is for all the red men to unite in claiming ... equal right in the land, as it was at first, and should be yet; for it never was divided, but belongs to all for the use of **each**. ...'

'... At that time the "gold fever" was contagious and few, old or young, escaped the malady. On the streets, in the fields, in the workshops and by the fireside, golden California was the chief topic of conversation. Who were going? How was best to "fix up" the outfit? What to take as food and clothing? Who would stay at home to care for the farm and womenfolks? Who would take wives and children along? Advice was handed out quite free of charge and often quite free of common sense. ...'

ORIGINS
NATIVE AMERICANS

When Europeans first arrived in the West, more than 200 Native American peoples already lived there. Peoples from the same region often had similar ways of life, so experts group them together in culture areas. There are 10 of these areas in North America, of which six are in the West (see map).

The Great Plains grasslands stretch from the Mississippi River to the Rocky Mountains. Plains people such as the Mandan were farmers, but most, like the Sioux, lived by hunting buffalo. People ate buffalo meat, made clothes and tipis from the hides, and carved tools from the bones.

The Great Basin is a high desert region enclosed by the Rocky Mountains and the Sierra Nevada. There the Ute and other peoples were hunter-gatherers, collecting plants and trapping animals such as groundhogs. Many Great Basin peoples lived

CULTURE AREAS

A Sioux village, by George Catlin

in conical, willow-wood frames covered with reeds or brush, called wickiups.

The High Plateau contains deserts, pine forests and grasslands. Deep canyons carved out by the Columbia and Fraser rivers cut across its landscape. Plateau peoples such as the Nez Percé were hunter-

gatherers, too, whose main food was salmon. They lived in wooden, mud-covered pit-houses in winter and flimsy reed lodges in summer.

The peoples of the California culture area were also hunter-gatherers. Coastal groups, including the Chumash, lived mainly on fish, such as tuna and halibut. Their houses varied from temporary, redwood-bark shelters to more permanent, thatched wooden huts.

The mountains, rivers and cedar forests of the Pacific Northwest provided a home for peoples such as the Tlingit. Salmon and other fish were their principal food, but they also hunted animals such as deer, and gathered plants. They built houses and totem poles from cedarwood.

The Southwest culture area is largely desert. However, the Hopi, Zuni and other Pueblo peoples knew how to irrigate the land, and grew crops such as maize. They used adobe brick to build their villages and towns. At some time between AD1200 and 1400, the Navajo and Apache migrated into the region from the north. These warlike peoples lived mainly by hunting and raiding Pueblo settlements.

Despite their varied lifestyles, the Native American peoples had much in common. In particular, they all believed that a supernatural spirit world affected their everyday lives. And they shared a deep attachment to their homelands.

MOVING IN

The first inhabitants of North America, the ancestors of the Native Americans, walked there from Siberia in Asia during the last Ice Age. At that time, a bridge of land known as Beringia linked the continents. Historians suggest that the migrations took place between about 40,000 and 12,000 years ago.

Native Americans' religious beliefs reflect their deep sense of belonging to their environment. Many of their creation stories tell how the gods made everything – people, animals, plants and the natural features of their homelands. The Blackfeet, a buffalo-hunting people of the Great Plains, tell this story:

Blackfeet people, by George Catlin

The name for the god whom the Blackfeet believe created them.

The Teton (Milk) River runs through the state of Montana.

'**Old Man** was traveling about ... making the people ... animals and birds ... mountains, prairies, timber and brush ... He made the **Milk River** and ... lay down to rest. As he lay on his back, ... he marked himself out with stones – the shape of his body, head, legs, arms, and everything. There you can see those rocks today. After he had rested, he went on northward, and stumbled ... and fell down on his knees. Then he said, "You are a bad thing to be stumbling against"; so he raised up two large **buttes** there, and named them the Knees, and they are called so to this day. He went on farther north, and with some of the rocks he carried with him he built the Sweet Grass Hills.'

A butte is a flat-topped, rocky hill.

THE ARRIVAL OF THE SPANISH

On 12 October 1492, Italian explorer Christopher Columbus landed on an island in the Bahamas. He believed that he had reached Asia, but in fact he was off the coast of Florida. This was the first of Columbus's four voyages to the Americas, funded by King Ferdinand and Queen Isabella of Spain. Reports of his success brought many Spaniards to try their luck in the New World.

Spanish *conquistadors* explored Central and South America and discovered the wealthy Aztec and Inca civilisations. Rumours spread that great riches awaited explorers in North America too. From 1540 to 1542 Francisco Vásquez de Coronado led about 300 people, including at least three women, across what is now New Mexico,

Santa Clara de Asis mission, California, in the 18th century (see page 11)

Arizona, Texas and Kansas. They clashed violently with the Pueblo peoples (see pages 8-9), but found little gold or silver.

In 1598, Juan de Oñate led about 130 soldiers and their families north into New Mexico, to claim the land for Spain. He set up the first permanent European colonies in the American West. The Pueblo peoples there were

forced to convert to Roman Catholicism, to build missions and to work on the mission farms. They were taught to grow European crops of wheat, peaches and figs, and to look after European animals, such as horses, sheep and cattle.

By the late 17th century, the Pueblo peoples were in a desperate state. The Catholic priests were suppressing their religious beliefs with increasing violence, and European diseases had reduced their population to half its original size of over 30,000. Years of drought brought poor harvests and starvation, and Navajo and Apache warriors raided their weakened communities. In 1680, the Pueblo peoples revolted. Led by a man called El Popé, they drove the Spanish

In 1599, Juan de Oñate's forces conquered the Acoma Pueblo with great violence. Their city is seen here, perched high on rocks in what is now New Mexico.

from New Mexico against all odds. However, between 1692 and 1696, another Spaniard, Diego de Vargas, reconquered the area.

Soon afterwards, the Spanish expanded into Arizona and elsewhere. From 1716 they set up *presidios* (forts) in Texas as a defence against the French, who had colonised Louisiana to the east (see pages 12-13). In 1769, they began to establish *presidios* and missions in California, to prevent the Russians and the English from taking over their territories in the West. Among these Californian settlements were San Francisco and Los Angeles.

FIRST IN THE WEST

Coronado was not the first European in the West. In 1528, Alvar Núñez Cabeza de Vaca, commanding about 40 soldiers and slaves, was sailing back to Mexico after a failed attempt to conquer Florida for Spain. Their ship was wrecked on the Texas coast, and they were forced to continue over land. Only four of them survived the journey. Nevertheless, Cabeza de Vaca's reports of their adventures fuelled Spanish interest in the West and encouraged the later expeditions.

Coronado wrote in Spanish. This first English version of his letters was published in 1600.

When he reached the pueblos of New Mexico in 1540, Coronado realised that the rumours about fabulously rich places, such as the Seven Cities of Cibola, were probably myths. He wrote this letter to the viceroy, or governor, of New Spain in August 1540:

Turquoises are a type of gemstone. Coronado and the other members of his expedition were looking for jewels as well as precious metals.

' ... The Seven Cities are seven little villages...In this place where I am now lodged there are perhaps 200 houses, all surrounded by a wall ... there might be altogether 500 families. ...The people of the towns seem ... of ordinary size and intelligent...They all have good figures, and are well bred. I think that they have a quantity of **turquoises**, which they had removed with the rest of their goods, except the **corn**, when I arrived ... Two points of emerald and some little broken stones which approach the color of rather poor garnets were found in a paper ...

Corn (maize) formed a major part of the Pueblo peoples' diet.

EUROPEAN RIVALRY

Tales of the imagined riches of North America attracted people of many other nations apart from Spain. From the 16th to the 18th centuries, the most important of these were France and Britain. They became great rivals, and their activities were to have lasting consequences for the future of the West.

Like Columbus, the French explorer Jacques Cartier was looking not only for riches, but also for a sea route to Asia. During 1534 and again in 1542, he travelled along and around the St Lawrence River, but he found neither. However, he noted that the region was home to many fur-bearing animals such as beavers. His reports encouraged the French to trade in furs with local Native Americans. This developed into an important business that spread far into the West (see pages 18-19).

In 1603 another Frenchman, Samuel de Champlain, arrived in eastern Canada and claimed the region for his country. Fur trader Sieur René de la Salle extended French influence southwards when he travelled down the Mississippi River to the Gulf of Mexico from 1679 to 1682. On completing his journey he claimed a vast territory on either side of the river for France and called it Louisiana. The French began to colonise the area in the following century, and soon posed a threat both to the Spanish in the West and the British in the East.

The first permanent British settlement in North America was established in Jamestown, Virginia, in 1607. By 1733, thirteen British colonies occupied land along the east coast. Britain also claimed an area of Canada known as Rupert's Land, although the French disputed this. In 1763, Britain defeated France in the Seven Years' War (1756-1763). The Treaty of Paris, which ended the war, gave Canada, Florida and all land east of the Mississippi River to Britain. France gave Louisiana west of the Mississippi to Spain.

Britain enjoyed its success for only a short time. In 1775 the American Revolution began, during which the 13 British colonies rebelled against the government in London. In 1776,

The Declaration of Independence, in which the original 13 states of the USA officially broke away from British rule.

they proclaimed themselves an independent nation – the United States of America. Some pioneers had already ventured beyond colonial boundaries (see pages 14-15). After independence, many more turned their eyes westwards.

Native Americans received knives, guns and other goods in return for furs.

RUSSIAN AMERICA

In 1740, Danish explorer Vitus Bering set off on a voyage sponsored by the Tsar of Russia. He came to Kayak Island off the coast of Alaska and noticed that the local people caught sea otters for their beautiful fur. Bering died on the voyage, but his crew reported their findings to the tsar. Soon, Russian hunters headed for Alaska to trap sea otters for themselves.

In 1799, Russian Alexander Baranov set up a fort in New Archangel (modern Sitka), Alaska. Following its invasion by Tlingits (see pages 8-9), a second fort was built in 1804. The Russian fur trade flourished. The Russians' trading rivals were the British, who also traded in sea otter pelts.

The Tlingit still tell stories about the day Russians arrived in their strange foreign ship. This extract describes how the Tlingit tried to make sense of the event by relating it to their religious beliefs.

Tlingit clothes were often beautifully decorated, like this shirt.

Raven, the Trickster, was a main character in Tlingit religion. In one story, he drops stones from his beak into the waters that once covered the world. In this way, land was formed.

'At one point one morning
a person went outside.
Then there was a white object that
  could be seen
way out on the sea
bouncing on the waves
and rocked by the waves.
At one point it was coming closer to
  the people.
"What's that?"
"What's that, what's that?"
"It's something different!"
"It's something different!"
"It's something different!"
"Is it Raven?"
"Maybe that's what it is."
"I think that's what it is-
Raven who created the world.
He said he would come back again."'

ACROSS THE APPALACHIANS

After the Seven Years' War (1756-1763), Britain gained French lands west of the Appalachians (see pages 12-13). The British government did not want to provoke the Native Americans there, as many had fought on the French side and remained hostile. So it set up a Proclamation Line, which non-Native Americans were forbidden to cross. However, Americans were already resisting British rule and many disregarded the Line, heading west. Farmers and speculators wanted free land, while traders hoped to profit from fur-trapping.

In 1783, Britain recognised the independence of the United States and gave up its territory beyond the Appalachians. More people flocked westwards, while existing states tried to claim the new land. The US government divided the area into Northwest and Southwest Territories, and passed two major land laws.

The Land Ordinance of 1785 divided the territories into sections of 1 square mile, to be auctioned singly or as 36-section townships. The Northwest Ordinance of 1787 divided that territory into smaller territories and allowed each to apply for statehood once its population reached 60,000. By 1802, the entire region was under federal government control.

THE USA IN THE EARLY 19TH CENTURY

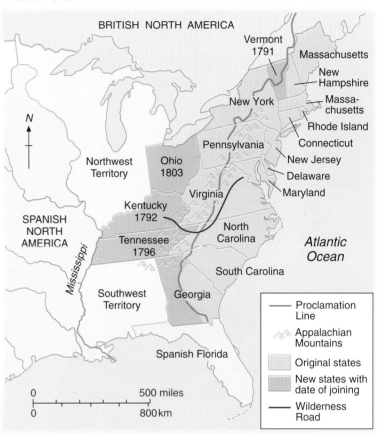

BRITISH NORTH AMERICA

Vermont 1791
Massachusetts
New Hampshire
New York
Massa-chusetts
Rhode Island
Pennsylvania
Connecticut
New Jersey
Northwest Territory
Ohio 1803
Delaware
Virginia
Maryland
Kentucky 1792
SPANISH NORTH AMERICA
North Carolina
Tennessee 1796
Atlantic Ocean
South Carolina
Mississippi
Southwest Territory
Georgia

Spanish Florida

N

0   500 miles
0   800 km

——	Proclamation Line
⌃⌃⌃	Appalachian Mountains
▨	Original states
▨	New states with date of joining
——	Wilderness Road

Some people crossed the Appalachians by the rough Wilderness Road carved out by Daniel Boone. They poured through the Cumberland Gap and settled in the region of modern Kentucky. Others took the National Road, which opened in 1818. People also travelled by water, down the Ohio River or along the Erie Canal. This canal, completed in 1825, crossed New York State from Albany to Buffalo on the shores of Lake Erie.

Pioneer families slowly made new lives. They cut down trees for log cabins and planted crops such as corn, potatoes and pumpkins on the cleared ground. They raised children, who were expected to do their share of the work, as well as keep up with lessons. Clothes were made from animal skins, wool, cotton and linen. Many settlers kept pigs,

Daniel Boone leads settlers through the Cumberland Gap into Kentucky, by George Bingham, 1852

A cabin built with logs and a turf roof

THE LEATHERSTOCKING TALES

Some of the earliest pioneers were hunters and fur-trappers. Their story, part-myth, part-reality, lives on. American author James Fenimore Cooper wrote five books about one fictional pathfinder, Natty Bumppo, nicknamed Leatherstocking. In tales such as *The Last of the Mohicans* (1826), Leatherstocking lives a wild, free life in the woods, befriending and coming into conflict with Native Americans.

cows and sheep, and hunted other animals such as raccoons and turkeys. Some pioneers moved further west, looking for a better life. Others remained, gradually turning forest into ploughed farmland and growing more crops than they needed, so that the surplus could be sold at market.

THE
DISCOVERY, SETTLEMENT
And prefent State of
KENTUCKE:
AND
An ESSAY towards the TOPOGRAPHY, and NATURAL HISTORY of that important Country:
To which is added,
An APPENDIX,
CONTAINING,
I. The ADVENTURES of Col. *Daniel Boon*, one of the firft Settlers, comprehending every important Occurrence in the political Hiftory of that Province.
II. The MINUTES of the *Piankafhaw* council, held at *Poft St. Vincents*, April 15, 1784.
III. An ACCOUNT of the *Indian* Nations inhabiting within the Limits of the Thirteen United States, their Manners and Cuftoms, and Reflections on their Origin.
IV. The STAGES and DISTANCES between *Philadelphia* and the Falls of the *Ohio*; from *Pittfburg* to *Penfacola* and feveral other Places. —The Whole illuftrated by a new and accurate MAP of *Kentucke* and the Country adjoining, drawn from actual Surveys.
By JOHN FILSON.
Wilmington, Printed by JAMES ADAMS, 1784.

Daniel Boone, a farmer and fur-trapper from Carolina, was an early explorer of Kentucky. In 1775 he and 500 men built the Wilderness Road, and set up the town of Boonesborough near the Kentucky River.
***The Discovery, Settlement and Present State of Kentucke* by John Filson, published in 1784, describes Boone as a visionary rather than the down-to-earth character he probably was. This extract describes an adventure during the construction of the Wilderness Road.**

'... We proceeded with all possible **expedition** until we came within fifteen miles of where Boonsborough now stands, and where we were fired upon by a party of **Indians**. . . . Three days after, we were fired upon again, and had two men killed, and three wounded. Afterwards we proceeded on to Kentucke river without opposition; and on the first day of April began to erect the fort of Boonsborough at a **salt lick**, about sixty yards from the river, on the S. side...'

'expedition' here means 'speed'.

Using money borrowed from businessmen, Boone had purchased the road site from the Cherokee people. But he and his men still suffered constant attacks.

A salt lick is a narrow area of land with deposits of salt on its surface.

THE LOUISIANA PURCHASE

In 1803, the USA under President Thomas Jefferson purchased the huge new territory of Louisiana – 770,000 square miles – from the French for $15 million. As a result, the USA more than doubled in size, and became much stronger in relation to Spain, which still occupied large areas of the West. The next stage in the westward expansion of the USA had begun.

Jefferson was delighted with the Louisiana Purchase for other reasons, too. He hoped to find a route from the eastern states to the Pacific Ocean. This would enable Americans to sail direct to Asia and to profit from the coastal fur trade. Jefferson believed that it might be possible to sail west along Louisiana's Missouri River, cross the Rocky

THE LOUISIANA PURCHASE

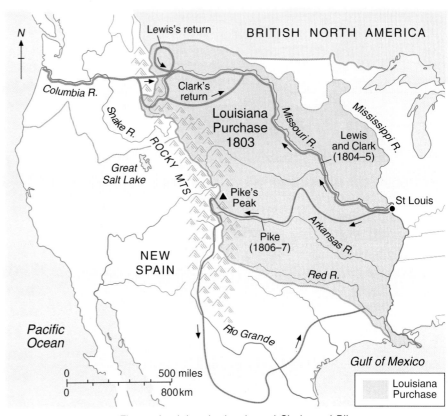

The routes taken by Lewis and Clark, and Pike

Jefferson signs the Louisiana Purchase

Mountains, then follow another river such as the Columbia to the ocean. The President also had some scientific curiosity – he wanted to learn more about the peoples, plants, animals and landscape of the West.

In 1803, Jefferson commissioned an army officer, Meriwether Lewis, to lead the Missouri River expedition. Lewis, with officer William Clark and about 46 men – the Corps of Discovery – left St Louis in May 1804. Nearing the end of the Missouri River, in August 1805, they realised that there was no direct river route across North America. Enduring great hardship, the Corps crossed the Rocky Mountains, on foot and on horseback. With the help of the Shoshone people, they found the Columbia River. Travelling along this waterway, they reached the Pacific in November 1805, and by September 1806 were back in St Louis.

The Louisiana Purchase and the Lewis and Clark Expedition made the West a reality in the minds of many Americans. But it was some time before any but the adventurous few dared to go there.

 Lewis and Clark recorded their 8,000 mile expedition in journals (see below). The extract below (right) tells how a Shoshone woman, Sacagawea, showed the explorers which plants were safe to eat. She also guided them through difficult terrain. Her help contributed to the expedition's success.

A page from Lewis and Clark's journal

PIKE'S PEAK

Lewis and Clark were not the only early explorers of Louisiana. In 1805, Lieutenant Zebulon Montgomery Pike was sent to find the source of the Mississippi River, which marked the eastern boundary of the new territory. A year later, he led an expedition to the Arkansas and Red Rivers in the south-west. In so doing, Pike roamed across Spanish land and was taken prisoner on suspicion of being a spy. Even today, historians are not sure if he really was, but he was soon set free. Pike is best remembered for becoming the first European to map a 14,000 ft mountain in Colorado. It is now called Pike's Peak.

Sacagawea guides the Corps of Discovery

TUESDAY APRIL 9Th (1805)

'... when we halted for dinner [Sacagawea] busied herself in serching for the wild artichokes which the mice collect and deposit in large hoards. this operation she performed by penetrating the earth with a sharp stick about some small collections of drift wood. her labour soon proved successful, and she procured a good quantity of these roots ...'

THE FUR TRADE

The French, British and Russians had been growing rich from the fur trade for many years. During the 16th century, French fur traders, called *coureurs de bois* or 'forest runners', had worked with Native Americans to trap beavers. But in the 17th century, large companies began to move in on their territory. The British Hudson's Bay Company, founded in 1670, operated across much of northern North America. Its main rival was the Canadian-controlled North West Fur Company, established in 1783. The Russians, like the British, were heavily involved in the sea otter trade.

William Clark himself set up one of the earliest American fur companies. In 1809, along with Spanish merchant Manuel Lisa, he formed the Missouri Fur Company in St Louis. German-born, New York businessman John Jacob Astor founded the Pacific Fur Company in 1810, and set up Astoria, a trading post on the Columbia River.

The diagram's inner circle shows the trapper's activities. The outer circle shows the annual cycle of the beaver.

Beaver traps were set on land or in the water.

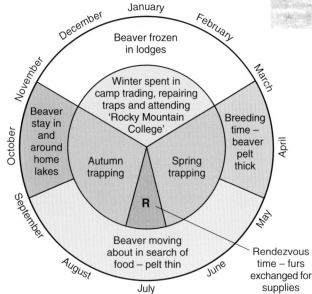

The Rocky Mountain Fur Company was founded by General William Henry Ashley in 1822. Ashley funded an expedition to search for an overland route through the Rockies. He chose Jedediah Strong Smith to lead the expedition. Smith discovered South Pass and huge colonies of beaver.

Smith was among the first of the adventurers who became known as mountain men. They came from many backgrounds. Smith himself was a devout Methodist from New York State, James Bridger had been a blacksmith in Missouri, while

Jim Beckwourth was an African American and former slave from Virginia. As well as trapping for furs, these men explored many areas of the West unknown to non-Native Americans.

The main fur-trapping seasons were spring and autumn. In winter, beavers stayed in their lodges and mountain men in their camps. In summer, gatherings known as *rendezvous* were held. Here, trappers and Native Americans sold the pelts they had collected to the fur companies. These meetings were also times of wild partying and sometimes fighting. However, in the 1840s, beaver fur went out of fashion and the fur trade declined.

ROCKY MOUNTAIN COLLEGE

Mountain men lived a harsh life. They endured mountain blizzards, grizzly bear attacks and Native American raids. They frequently spent weeks alone with little to eat and only their rifles to protect them. Their dress – often a fur hat and buckskin suit – also marked them out as strangers to polite society. Yet in winter, many of them went to 'Rocky Mountain College'. This was not an institution or building, but time spent reading, or in many cases learning to read. Among the most popular books were schoolroom favourites such as William Shakespeare's plays and Sir Walter Scott's novels.

American artist Alfred Jacob Miller visited a Rocky Mountain rendezvous in 1837. He not only painted the bustling scene, but also recorded the following description of it in his notebook:

'Fur trappers at the Rendezvous' by Alfred Jacob Miller

'... At certain specified times during the year, the **American Fur Company** appoint a 'Rendezvous' at particular localities (selecting the most available spots) for the purpose of trading with **Indians** and Trappers, and here they congregate from all quarters. The first day is devoted to 'High Jinks'... feasting, drinking, and gambling ...The following days ... The Fur Company's great tent is raised; the Indians erect their picturesque **white lodges**; the accumulated furs of the hunting season are brought forth and the Company's tent is a besieged and busy place. ...'

The American Fur Company was John Jacob Astor's first fur business, founded in 1808.

Native Americans

These were buffalo-hide tipis.

INDIAN REMOVAL

Following the Louisiana Purchase in 1803, the USA adopted a policy of moving eastern Native American peoples west of the Mississippi River. They were encouraged to live more like white people. Two Shawnee brothers, Tecumseh and Tenskwatawa, warned the peoples that if they did not resist, white settlement would spread and Native American cultures would collapse.

On 7 November 1811, William Henry Harrison, governor of the Indiana Territory, led an army against the brothers and their supporters, and defeated them at the Battle of Tippecanoe. Tecumseh then allied with the British, who in 1812 were again at war with the Americans. But in 1813, he was killed.

Others continued the struggle, but in 1814, an army led by future president Andrew Jackson defeated the southeastern Creek people at the Battle of Horseshoe Bend. In 1815, the British withdrew from the northeast.

Shawnee brothers Tenskwatawa (left) and Tecumseh

From this time on, Native American peoples throughout the east were forced to sign treaties in which they granted their lands to whites and agreed to settle in reservations west of the Mississippi.

Andrew Jackson became president in 1829. Southern states such as Georgia wanted Native American land for cotton plantations, and in 1830, the Indian Removal Bill was passed. The Act gave land beyond the Mississippi to Native Americans, forcing eastern peoples to move there. If they did not, the government said it would not protect them from anti-Native American laws made by individual states. Faced with this prospect, many peoples set out for the West, only to starve on land they could not cultivate. From 1831 to 1832, the Sac and Fox Native Americans of Illinois fought to remain on their lands, but were finally defeated.

Some of the southeastern tribes also resisted, particularly the Cherokee, who had adopted a white American way of life and argued that they should not be removed. In 1835, some Cherokee did sign a removal treaty, but since no elected Cherokee leader was present, many still refused to leave. In 1838, government troops forced

Following his victory at the Battle of Tippecanoe (left), William Henry Harrison became known as 'Tippecanoe'. His success continued, and in 1840 he became President of the United States.

them out. On the trek west about 4000 Cherokee died, and their journey is known as the 'Trail of Tears'.

White settlers continued to pour west. By 1840, a third of the American population lived between the Appalachian Mountains and the Mississippi River.

INDIAN TERRITORY

The US Congress set aside a huge area of land west of the Mississippi for Native American settlement and in 1834 named it Indian Territory. (The white settlers called all the Native American peoples 'Indians'.) It covered the modern states of Kansas and Oklahoma, parts of Nebraska, Colorado and Wyoming. Historians estimate that about 90,000 Native Americans moved there. Some of the peoples who already lived there objected – Comanche, Cheyenne and other warriors attacked the newcomers. In some cases, government troops had to restore order.

 Tecumseh visited Governor Harrison of Indiana in 1810 to plead for just treatment of Native Americans. He was a powerful speaker:

Many Native Americans believed that a powerful spirit flowed through all living creatures and influenced their actions.

'red men' here means Native Americans.

Native Americans did not think in terms of owning land. It was freely available to all, like the air.

'... The **being within**, communing with past ages, tells me that ... until lately, there was no white man on this continent. ... all belonged to **red men**, ... placed on it by the **Great Spirit** ... Once a happy race. Since made miserable by the white people, who are never contented but always encroaching. The way ... to stop this evil, is for all the red men to unite in claiming ... equal right in the land, as it was at first, and should be yet; for it never was divided, but **belongs to all for the use of each**. ...'

President Andrew Jackson

This phrase became infamous, because Jackson's promise proved completely untrue.

At the time of the Indian Removal, President Jackson sent an army officer to explain his policies to the Cherokee and Choctaw peoples, in these words:

'Say to the chiefs and warriors that I ... wish to act as their friend but they must, by removing from ... Mississippi and Alabama and by being settled on the lands I offer them, put it in my power to be such ... There, beyond the limits of any State, in possession of land of their own, which they shall possess **as long as Grass grows or water runs**, I am and will protect them and be their friend and father...'

WESTWARD EXPANSION

In the Adams-Onis Treaty of 1819, Spain gave up Florida, acquired from the British in 1783, and abandoned claims to the Pacific coast north of California. In 1821, it was forced to grant independence to Mexico, which then became ruler of Spain's former lands in the North American West.

Among these lands was Texas. In an attempt to bring wealth to the region, the new Mexican rulers encouraged trade with the USA. They also granted land to rich American colonisers, known as *empresarios*. For every 25,000 acres they received, the colonisers had to bring 100 American families across the border to farm. The first *empresario* was Stephen F. Austin, after whom the Texan state capital is named. Thousands of individual Americans also bought cheap land.

By 1835, about 35,000 Americans lived in Texas, and disputes flared over taxes, religion and slavery. The Mexicans had banned slavery, but many Americans supported it. In 1835 violence erupted, and on 2 March 1836, Americans in Texas declared the region's independence.

On 6 March, 2600 soldiers led by Mexican ruler General Antonio López de Santa Anna attacked the Alamo fortress (see map). Most of its 187 defenders were killed, but eight men, including politician and hunter Davy Crockett, were later executed. On 21 April, Americans led by

The fall of the Alamo

WESTWARD EXPANSION

The USA expanded after 1819, when Spain gave up Florida and land north of the Adams-Onis line. Territory won from Mexico in the wars of 1846-48 was extended in the Gadsden Purchase of 1853.

General Sam Houston crushed the Mexicans at the Battle of San Jacinto. Santa Anna was then forced to accept the independence of Texas and the extension of its boundaries. Texas remained independent until 1845, when it became a state of the USA.

Mexicans never accepted Texans' right to the extra land they had claimed in 1836. In 1846, US President James K. Polk decided to resolve this question by force, hoping to acquire Mexican territory in California as well. The Mexican War lasted until 1848, when Mexico gave the USA all its land north of the Rio Grande – about 500,000 square miles – in return for $15 million.

By this time, the USA had also extended its boundaries up the Pacific coast. The Americans had ruled Oregon jointly with the British since 1818. After long negotiations under President Polk, the territory was divided between the two countries in 1846, the USA taking the southern section.

Army officer John Charles Frémont explored the West. He also played an important part in the Mexican War.

THE SANTA FE TRAIL

In 1821, merchant William Becknell set out from Independence in Missouri for Santa Fe, New Mexico. The 800 mile path he followed, known as the Santa Fe Trail, became an important trading route. Wagon trains from the USA (see below) carried a huge variety of goods, from blankets and shawls to glass and knives. They returned full of furs, gold and silver, and with valuable Spanish horses.

Many US citizens believed their country had a God-given right to settle North America. In 1845, John L. O'Sullivan, editor of the *United States Magazine and Democratic Review*, called this belief 'manifest destiny'. O'Sullivan complained that other nations were meddling:

' ... for the avowed object of thwarting our policy and hampering our power, limiting our greatness and checking the fulfillment of our manifest destiny to overspread the continent allotted by Providence for the free development of our yearly multiplying millions ...'

'Providence' here means 'God'.

CHAPTER 2

HEADING WEST
ACROSS THE MISSISSIPPI

In 1837, an economic depression hit the East and Midwest, causing poverty and unemployment. At the same time, people were reading books by explorers and missionaries who painted an enticing picture of the Far West. The idea of 'manifest destiny' had also taken hold (see pages 22-23), as well as a longing for land and adventure.

In 1843, the period of the 'Great Migration' west to Oregon and California began. In that year, about 1000 people journeyed west in wagons, on horseback and on foot. A year later, still more people set out on the California and Oregon Trails.

The 2,000 mile trek began each year in April, when migrants congregated around one of three 'jumping-off places' on the Missouri River – Independence, St Joseph or Council Bluffs.

For the first 1,200 miles, travellers to Oregon and California took the same route, crossing the Kansas plains to Fort Kearney, then following the River Platte to the fur-trading post of Fort Laramie. They crossed the Rocky Mountains by the South Pass. Beyond the mountains, the trails parted at Fort Hall. Migrants bound for Oregon headed north, many settling in the hospitable

THE OREGON AND CALIFORNIA TRAILS

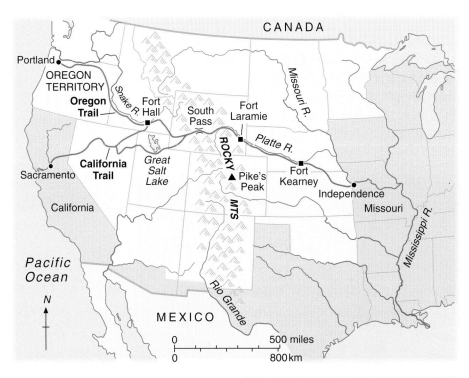

Willamette Valley. Those heading for California followed the Humboldt River to the Sacramento Valley. The journey was usually over by October, before the harsh winter snows. By 1860, some 260,000 people had made this journey.

As Midwestern farmers headed for the Far West, many newcomers settled in the Midwest. From 1840 to 1860, 4.2 million people arrived in the USA. Many were Irish families forced from home by famine, who mostly stayed in the East. However, many Germans, Danes, Norwegians and Swedes

THE PREEMPTION BILL
American government surveyors could not keep pace with the migrations of the 1840s, so farmers squatted on unsurveyed territory. When this land was sold, speculators often paid higher prices than the farmers who were working the land could afford. In 1841, the government's Preemption Bill ended this injustice, giving settlers the right to squat on unsurveyed land and to purchase it at a low price.

California and Oregon

Most people travelled west in family groups, supporting one another along the way. Some people were adventurous and set out gladly. Others did not want to leave the lives that they knew. Mary A Jones was a reluctant traveller:

'... In the winter of 18 and 46 our neighbor ... began talking of moving to the New Country & brought [Frémont's] book to my husband to read, & he was carried away with the idea too. I said O let us not go ... but it made no difference ... We sold our home and what we could not take with us and what we could not sell...we gave away & on the 7th day of May 1846 we joined the camp for California. ...'

A romantic view of a wagon train, painted by F.O.C. Darley

Francis Parkman was a 19th-century American historian who wrote about the wars between the French and the British on American soil. He also published *The Oregon Trail* (1849), a record of his trip from Missouri to Oregon in 1846. In this extract, he describes seeing his first wagon train.

'caravan' here means 'wagon train'.

Parkman had left St Joseph on the Missouri River only eight days before. It would be many weeks before he reached Fort Hall, where the California and Oregon Trails divided.

'... we saw, far in advance of us, drawn against the horizon, a line of objects stretching at regular intervals along the level edge of the prairie ... a quarter of an hour afterwards we saw close before us the emigrant caravan, with its heavy white wagons creeping on in slow procession, and a large drove of cattle following behind ... As we approached they called out to us: "How are ye, boys? Are ye for Oregon or California?" ...'

LIFE ON THE OVERLAND TRAIL

A family on the trail

Careful preparation was necessary for life on the overland trail. In the early days, many pioneers travelled in Conestoga wagons. These were more than 23 ft long and weighed almost 3400 lbs. Their size made them difficult to manoeuvre, so people began to use smaller, lighter 'prairie schooners'. These had iron tires, timber frameworks and canvas covers stretched over hoops of hickory wood. Like the Conestogas, they were pulled by horses, oxen or mules.

The overlanders packed enough supplies to last for the six-month journey. They stored huge amounts of flour, butter, sugar, yeast, salt, tea, coffee and bacon in the wagons, as well as canned meat, fish and fruit. Women used all their cooking skills, rising before dawn to prepare the fire and to make bread, cakes and stews.

The pioneers also packed all the clothing that they would need. Men took several shirts and pairs of linsey-woolsey trousers, as well as a thick overcoat for cold weather. At first, most women took full-length woollen dresses, but these were impractical. Later on, women wore shorter dresses that did not touch the ground. Some women even dared to wear the newly fashionable 'bloomers'. Clothes had to be kept clean and in good repair. Some people chose special days for washing, others waited until their wagon stopped near a river.

The migrants encountered many hardships and problems. It was difficult for leaders to keep order, especially in large trains of more than 100 wagons. Outbreaks of cholera and other diseases left thousands dead and lines of makeshift graves along the routes. Terrifying, too, were the blizzards that whirled snow around the wagons and could suffocate the animals.

Many overlanders' greatest fear, however, was of attack by hostile peoples such as the Sioux. Adults carried guns to

A sketch showing wagons placed in a ring for safety

protect themselves and their children. At night, they arranged the wagons in a ring and armed guards kept watch. Soldiers were also on hand to come to the overlanders' rescue. During part of the 1850s, about 90 per cent of the US Army was stationed west of the Mississippi. In fact, the threat of attack was greatly overestimated. Of the 10,000 overlanders who died on the trails, about 400 were killed by Native Americans.

TRAIL TRASH

Western films often show wagon trains winding through beautiful scenery. They usually miss out a less picturesque feature of the overland routes – rubbish. Many migrants left behind anything that they no longer needed, including worn-out clothes and broken-down wagons.

Many people published books to help migrants prepare for their life on the trail. This extract comes from *The Prairie Traveller, A Handbook for Overland Expeditions* (1863). It was written by Randolph B. Marcy, a soldier who had spent much time in the West.

'gutta-percha' is another rubber-like substance that comes from the tree of the same name.

'... Bacon should be packed in strong sacks of a hundred pounds to each; or, in very hot climates, put in boxes and surrounded with bran, which in a great measure prevents the fat from melting away ... Flour should be packed in stout double canvas sacks well sewed, a hundred pounds in each sack. Butter may be preserved by boiling it thoroughly, and skimming off the scum as it rises to the top until it is quite clear like oil. It is then placed in tin canisters and soldered up. Sugar may be well secured in India-rubber or gutta-percha sacks, or so placed in the wagon as not to risk getting wet.'

Butter prepared in this way is known as clarified butter.

Thousands of children and teenagers made the trek westwards. This extract is taken from a letter by Virginia Reed, who was 13 years old when she wrote it. It describes the prairie schooner in which her family crossed North America.

'... The entrance was on the side ... and one stepped into a small room ... in the center of the wagon. At the right and left were spring seats with comfortable high backs, where one could sit and ride ... In this little room was placed a tiny sheet-iron stove, whose pipe, running through the top of the wagon, was prevented by a circle of tin, from setting fire to the canvas cover. A board about a foot wide extended over the wheels on either side ... of the wagon, thus forming the foundation for a large and roomy second story in which were placed our beds. Under the spring seats were compartments in which were stored many articles ... such as a well filled work basket and a full assortment of medicines ...'

THE MORMON TRAIL

One group of pioneers moved West because they were persecuted in the East and wanted to establish a religious community elsewhere. They were members of the Church of Jesus Christ of Latter-Day Saints, known as Mormons.

In 1830, Joseph Smith of Palmyra, New York, published the *Book of Mormon*, a collection of religious writings. According to this book, ancient tribes from Jerusalem had once settled in North America, and Jesus Christ had visited the continent after his Resurrection. Smith believed that it was his task to revive an old, 'true' form of Christianity, and he founded a church.

Many people converted to his religion, but many more regarded it as blasphemous. Smith moved his church to the Midwest, setting up communities in Ohio and Missouri. But violence soon erupted against the new arrivals,

so they moved again, to Illinois. There they founded the town of Nauvoo.

In Nauvoo, the Mormons governed themselves and established their own militia. But Smith outraged many non-Mormons by practising polygamy, and he alienated many Mormons by refusing to consider anyone's views but his own. In 1844, Joseph and his brother Hyrum were imprisoned for stirring up a riot. On June 27 a mob broke into the jail, then shot and killed them both.

Joseph Smith was replaced by Brigham Young. He believed that Mormons should settle in the Far West, where they would be free to live as they chose. In 1846, about 12,000 Mormons set out on the trail to the Great Salt Lake Valley (in modern Utah). There Young hoped to establish a Mormon homeland, covering a huge area of the

Brigham Young

West, from Idaho to Arizona. It was to be called the state of Deseret.

Young's hopes were dashed. In 1848 the USA annexed Mexico's former territories in the West, which included the Great Salt Lake area (see pages 22-23). The government objected not only to the Mormons' practice of polygamy but also to their apparent disregard for

Salt Lake City, Utah, 1860s. It is still the headquarters of the Mormon Church.

American laws. In July 1857, President James Buchanan sent troops to Utah. As a result, the Mormons agreed to honour American laws in return for a pardon, and the government outlawed polygamy.

Despite all their difficulties, the Mormons managed to establish a highly successful community in the West. They were disciplined farmers who worked together to raise crops from the dry land.

THE MOUNTAIN MEADOWS MASSACRE

The 1857 conflict between Mormons and government troops, sometimes called the Mormon War, ended without bloodshed. But it did lead to tragedy. When Mormons heard that the army was approaching, they went into a state of high alert. In September 1857, a wagon train of pioneers from Arkansas and Missouri passed through their territory. Convinced that the travellers posed a threat, Mormons joined with Paiute Native Americans to attack. In Mountain Meadows on the California Trail, 120 migrants were killed.

According to Joseph Smith, an angel showed him where to find the writings which formed the Book of Mormon. Smith described meeting the angel:

'... He called me by name and said unto me ... that his name was Moroni, that God had work for me to do; .... He said there was a book deposited, written upon golden plates, giving an account of the former inhabitants of this continent ...

Joseph Smith

Mormons continued to walk to the West until 1869, when the railroad reached Utah (see pages 50-51). Samuel Langhorne Clemens, better known as Mark Twain, described a Mormon wagon train in his novel *Roughing It* (1872), a semi-autobiographical account of his life in the West during the 1860s. (See also pages 32-33.)

This translation of the Book of Mormon shows some of the strange language in which it was first written.

'... Just beyond the breakfast-station we overtook a Mormon emigrant train of thirty-three wagons; and tramping wearily along and driving their herd of loose cows, were dozens of coarse-clad and sad-looking men, women and children, who had walked ... day after day for eight lingering weeks ... They were dusty and uncombed, hatless, bonnetless and ragged, and they did look so tired!...'

THE RUSH FOR GOLD

In January 1848, James Marshall was building a sawmill, and noticed something glimmering on the bed of the American River. Gold! Word quickly spread, and by 1849 the California Gold Rush was in full swing.

Almost 90,000 would-be gold miners – the 'forty-niners' – arrived from all parts of the USA, Britain, Ireland, France, Mexico, China and Australia. Life in the mining camps was harsh. Men, and a few intrepid women, lived in tents or ramshackle wooden huts. Their diet was poor, their toilet facilities were unhygienic, and disease, especially dysentery, was rife. There was crime, drunkenness and fighting. The camp names, from Bedbug to Whiskey Flat, told all.

Early prospectors used a simple technique, known as panning, to search for gold. They dipped a metal pan into a river, removing some mud and water, then swirled the mixture around. The moving water washed the lighter particles of dirt away, leaving the heavier gold at the bottom. Miners also used cradles, long wooden boxes mounted on rockers. When pushed to and fro, they separated the precious metal from the mud.

Panning for gold

Makeshift mining like this did not last. By late 1850, most of the easily accessible river gold had gone. The only way to find more metal was to extract it from its original source – underground quartz ores. Large mining companies moved in with machinery for drilling, crushing and dissolving

Virginia City, Nevada, grew up after the discovery of the huge deposits of gold and silver called the Comstock Lode. (See box , page 31.). Tin miners from England brought their skills here to search for gold.

rock. Some prospectors remained in California and became company employees. Some moved on to new gold and silver mines elsewhere (see box below). Some went home.

The end of the California mining bonanza disappointed many. To some it also brought persecution. In 1850, California became a state. Gold grew scarce, so American prospectors tried to force out foreigners. The Foreign Miners Tax of 1850 required all non-American gold-seekers to pay a monthly tax of $20. Many left, but the 25,000 Chinese in the state remained, suffering insults and beatings. In 1882, the government passed the Chinese Exclusion Act, prohibiting further Chinese immigration.

MORE MINES

In 1859, Pike's Peak in Colorado was the site of another major gold strike. In Nevada the Comstock Lode (after Henry T.P. Comstock, who claimed the land where it was found) yielded $300-million of gold and silver in 20 years.

In the 1860s, mining began in Idaho and Montana. And in the 1870s, gold finds in Dakota Territory provoked the final bitter confrontations between the United States Army and the Sioux (also known as the Dakota) Native Americans (see pages 52-53).

Lured by the prospect of gold, Catherine Haun and her husband set out for California from Iowa in 1849. In her diaries, Catherine describes the excitement in her home town of Clinton as news of the gold discoveries spread.

'... At that time the "gold fever" was contagious and few, old or young, escaped the malady. On the streets, in the fields, in the workshops and by the fireside, golden California was the chief topic of conversation. Who were going? How was best to "fix up" the outfit? What to take as food and clothing? Who would stay at home to care for the farm and womenfolks? Who would take wives and children along? Advice was handed out quite free of charge and often quite free of common sense. ...'

The Major found a piece of bacon rind and making a fire of sage brush sticks and buffalo chips, cooked and ate it. The men seemed more tired and hungry than were we women.

Our only death on the journey occurred in this desert. The Canadian woman, Mrs. Lamore, suddenly sickened and died, leaving her two little girls and grief stricken husband. The halted a day to bury her and the infant that had lived but an hour, in this weird, lonely spot on God's footstool away, apparently, from everywhere and everybody.

The bodies were wrapped together in a bedcomforter and wound, quite mummy-fied, with a few yards of string that we made by tying together torn strips of a cotton dress skirt. A passage of the Bible (my own) was read; a prayer offered and "Nearer, My God to Thee" sung. Owing to the unusual surroundings the ceremony was very impressive. Every heart was touched and eyes full of tears as we lowered the body, coffinless, into the grave. There was no tombstone — why should there be — the poor husband and orphans could never hope to revisit the grave and to the world it was just one of the many hundreds that marked the trail of the argonaut.

This burial and one I witnessed at sea some years later made a lasting impression upon me and I always think of them when I attend a funeral; such a gruesome sensation was caused by the desolation. The immense, lonesome plain; the great fathomless ocean — how insignificant seems the human body when consigned to their cold embrace!

Upon this desert there grew a wild, poisonous parsnip. One day we found a stake with a tin cup tied to it, at the head of a grave. The cup had a piece bitten or cut out. There were what seemed to be four graves, but we were not sure whether bodies of persons who had been poisoned by eating the weed

TRANSPORT AND COMMUNICATIONS

Samuel F.B. Morse (see page 33)

By the 1850s, new roads, canals and vehicles had made travel across North America quicker and safer. They had also made it easier and more profitable to carry farm produce from west to east and factory goods in the opposite direction. But the mass migrations of the mid-19th century made better transport essential.

In 1858, John Butterfield and William G Fargo set up the Overland Mail Company to carry post and passengers from St Louis in Missouri to San Francisco in California, a 25-day journey. The horse- or mule-drawn stagecoaches they used became a common sight in the West. Stagecoach travellers paid $200 for the privilege of being jolted over bumpy roads day and night, often in fear of attack by Native Americans or outlaws. But despite the discomfort, the speed of this means of transport made it popular.

Butterfield, Fargo and Henry Wells ran a second business, Wells, Fargo and Company. From the 1850s, it operated stagecoach routes within California, and from the mid-1860s in many other parts of the West. Wells, Fargo also ran a banking service for miners, and its bustling offices were a feature of almost every Western town.

Russell, Majors, and Waddell was another important transport business. It was formed in 1855, mainly to carry food, animals and military supplies to the US forts in the West. This company also founded the Pony Express, in April 1860, to transport mail on horseback. Each relay rider galloped across a 75 mile section of the route from St Joseph, Missouri to Sacramento, California, and the entire 2,000 mile journey was completed in 10 days. Although efficient, the Pony Express lasted only until October 1861, when the telegraph reached San Francisco.

Stagecoaches travelled at around 8km per hour, but on rough ground they could be much slower.

Telegraph operators at work. A telegraph key, used to tap out the messages, can be seen on the desk.

In 1844, Samuel F.B. Morse perfected the transmission of messages along wires using coded electrical signals. By 1861, telegraph lines had been established across North America, allowing almost instant communication throughout the continent. Telegraph offices, run by companies such as the Western Union, sprang up in many towns. Telegraph operators punched out dot-and-dash Morse Code messages on special telegraph keys.

All these developments in transport and communications played their part in shaping the West. But the real revolution came with the arrival of the railroad (see pages 50-51).

Mark Twain painted this vivid picture of a Pony Express rider in *Roughing It* (see pages 28-29).

All Pony Express riders were young men and many were teenagers.

The true distance was probably 75 miles (120 km) rather than 50 miles (80 km).

RIVER TRANSPORT

Many early pioneers used flatboats (large rafts) to travel west along the Ohio River. The journey was slow and could be dangerous, especially if a boat ran into rapids. In 1807, American inventor Robert Fulton started a passenger service along the Hudson River using his steamboat, the *Clermont*. In 1811, steamboats reached the West when the *New Orleans* travelled down the Ohio and Mississippi Rivers from Pittsburgh to New Orleans. Soon there was steamboat traffic along these and many other waterways, carrying not only migrants, but also goods such as cotton.

Steamboats and a flatboat on the Mississippi River

'... The pony-rider was usually a **little bit of a man**, brimful of spirit and endurance. No matter what time of the day or night his watch came on, ... winter or summer, raining, snowing, hailing or sleeting, ... level straight road or a crazy trail over mountain crags and precipices, ... he must be always ready to leap into the saddle and be off like the wind! There was no idling-time for a pony-rider on duty. He rode **fifty miles** without stopping, by daylight, moonlight, starlight, or through the blackness of darkness – just as it happened.

CHAPTER 3

LIVING IN THE WEST

FARMS AND FARMERS

A family and their sod house in Nebraska

By 1850, most of the USA's 1.5 million farmers still lived east of the Mississippi. Some were beginning to cultivate land in California and Oregon, and some were raising cattle in Texas and New Mexico. But the Plains remained largely unsettled. The territory was known as the Great American Desert, and its barren ground was not inviting.

From about 1850, however, farming families began to make their way into this unknown region. Then, in 1862, the new Homestead Act turned this slow movement into a mass migration. In it, the government agreed to grant 160 acres of land to any American citizen willing to pay a $10-dollar registration fee and to live on and farm a plot for five years. By

1870, thousands of homesteaders had set up farms on the eastern prairie plains. Some had also ventured on to the arid high plains further to the west.

Plains-bound migrants were helped by the spread of the railroad. By 1860, there were railway lines in every eastern state. The government gave railroad companies land to encourage them to continue their lines westward. To make money and generate business, the companies advertised in the USA and Europe to persuade people to buy sections of their territory.

Plains settlement was happening at the time of another significant episode in American history – the Civil War (1861-1865). This bitter struggle

between northern and southern states was fought around the question of slavery, which the South supported and the North did not. Bloody fighting took place in the West, particularly in Kansas. The North's victory brought the abolition of slavery.

Life on the Plains demanded ingenuity and endurance. There were few trees for cabin-building, so people lived in dug-outs cut into hillsides or, later, sod houses made of turf bricks. Water was scarce on the western plains, where there were few rivers and little rain fell. The pioneers sank wells deep into the

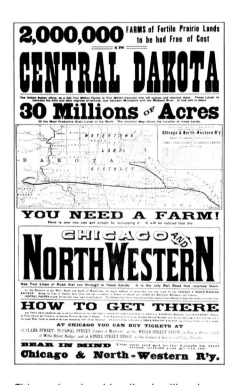

This poster aimed to attract settlers to Dakota. More settlers meant more business.

ground, then built windmills to pump water up to the surface.

Summer brought drought and locusts that devastated crops. Rain storms caused houses to collapse, lightning sparked prairie fires, and winter blizzards froze the ground solid. Tornadoes uprooted homes, while wind storms blew away the soil and filled the air with choking dust.

Every family member had to work hard to survive on the Plains. Men used steel ploughs (see box) to turn the heavy soil, dug wells and built windmills. Women worked on the land, too, and cooked, cleaned and made clothes without labour-saving devices. They also bore and raised children with little assistance from doctors or teachers. Everyone, including children, tended the animals. The early enthusiasm of some homesteaders faded, but others endured. Westward migration did not stop (see pages 54-55).

In 1863, during the Civil War, raiders from the south led by William Quantrill attacked the Kansas town of Lawrence. This eye-witness account of the event was recorded by anti-slavery campaigner Julia Lovejoy.

'... One lady threw her arms around her husband and begged of them to spare his life. They rested the pistol on her arm as it was around his body, and shot him dead, and the fire from the pistol burnt the sleeve of her dress. Mrs. Reed put out the fire six times to save her house, and they would fire it anew, but she by superhuman exertions saved it ... All the business houses, banks, stores, &c., in the city were robbed and burned save one, and most of the business men killed....'

FARM MACHINERY

Farmers between the Appalachians and the Mississippi used simple tools. The soft soil there could be turned by wooden ploughs with iron points, and hoes, sickles and axes served for most other tasks. From the 1830s, new machines revolutionised farming. The mechanical reaper, invented by Cyrus McCormick in 1831, harvested 100 acres in the time it took a reaper with a sickle to harvest eight. The blade of the steel plough, invented by John Deere in 1837, cut through the heavy Plains soil easily.

THE CATTLE KINGDOM

In the 1860s, large-scale cattle-ranching emerged on the Great Plains. There were several reasons for this. Cattle were left untended during the Civil War, and multiplied until about 5 million Texas longhorns roamed across the region. The American public had developed a taste for beef. Finally, the railroad had reached the eastern Plains.

Illinois livestock-buyer Joseph G. McCoy knew that Texas beef would sell for high prices in the east and north. He also realised that cattle could be transported to these markets by railroad. So he persuaded a railroad company to extend a track to Abilene, Kansas. Then he encouraged the small-scale farmers who already drove their cattle north each year to bring them to Abilene.

After the Civil War, many soldiers were unemployed. Some began to capture and farm the wild cattle. Others, together with many former slaves, such as Nat Love (right) signed up as cowboys to drive the cattle north. There were many Mexican cowboys around, who taught their new colleagues cattle-farming skills.

CATTLE TRAILS

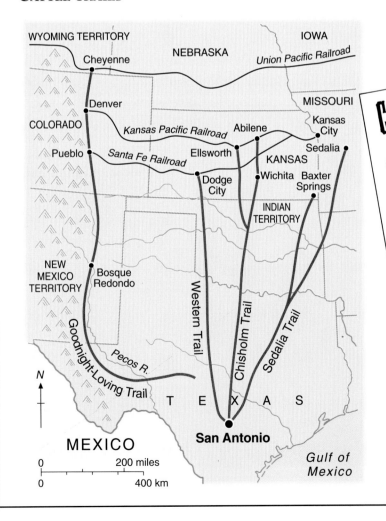

CATTLE MEN READ THIS!

Great Inducements to those who wish to

Ship Cattle on the U. P. Railroad!!

Having entered into special arrangements with the U. P. R. R. Company, by which I can ship Cattle East at greatly reduced rates, and having selected a point between Carter and Church Buttes Stations some ten miles East of the former place, near the junction of the Big and Little Muddies, and having Constructed Commodious Lots and Extensive Enclosures, and the Company having put in a Switch capable of holding 40 Cars, I will be Prepared to Commence Shipping on or before the 15th of the Present Month, and will be able to promptly ship any Number of cattle that may be Offered.

Persons driving Cattle from Montana and Idaho, and passing by Soda Springs and the Bear Lake Settlements, will cross over from Bear River to the head of Little Muddy and follow down that stream, over a good road to within a mile and a half of the junction of the Little with the Big Muddy, where they will cross a bridge and find a rich pasture, extending many miles; great water & perfect security for their stock, within convenient distance of the stock yards.

The cattle yards are in an enclosure of some 400 acres, and stock scales and all conveniences for shipping will be furnished. If parties do not wish to ship themselves, I will purchase, at good prices, all shipping cattle that may be offered. As cattle are now bearing excellent prices East, it would be well for persons to bring their Cattle forward as soon as possible.

For further particulars, address

W. A. CARTER,
Fort Bridger, Wyo. Ter.

From W. G. Joy Clerk, Operation Ogden, Utah.

Fort Bridger, July 2, 1877.

During McCoy's first year of operation, 1867, some 36,000 cattle were driven over the 500 miles from San Antonio, Texas to Abilene. By 1871, the number had risen to 700,000. A cow that cost $5 in Texas sold for $30 or more in Kansas. Cowboys' wages were low (see document) and the cows ate grass that grew freely on the open range. So profits were huge and the Cattle Kingdom of the Plains flourished.

The route to Abilene, known as the Chisholm Trail, was soon one of many (see map), and the long drives to the railheads became a feature of Western life. The drive usually began in spring and lasted for three or four months.

This 19th-century account of preparations for a cattle trail was written by Clarence W. Gordon, an agricultural agent in Texas.

The Goodnight-Loving Trail, founded by Charles Goodnight and Oliver Loving in 1866, led not to a railhead, but to the Navajo reservation at Bosque Redondo, where people were starving. Then it ran north to mining towns in Colorado and Wyoming. Goodnight wrote:

'... my years on the trail were the happiest I ever lived. There were many hardships and dangers, of course, that called on all a man had of endurance and bravery, but when all went well there was no other life so pleasant. Most of the time we were solitary adventurers in a great land as fresh and new as a spring morning, and we were free and full of the zest of darers....'

Cowboys gathered around their chuckwagon to eat, drink coffee, sing songs and tell stories about life on the trail.

'state' here refers to Texas.

'camp wagon' is another name for the chuck wagon, which carried food, water, medicines and other supplies for cowboys on the trail.

... Early in the year, the drover goes to that region of the **state** where he expects to find suitable stock and visits the various ranches. Having bought the cattle ... he goes to some horse ranch and buys ... say 40 horses for each average drove of 2,300 to 2,500 cattle. He also engages about a dozen cowboys for each such drove, at the rate of $25 to $30 per month, and a **"boss" drover** as field manager of the stock, equipment, and men, at $90 per month. Having made these engagements, and purchased a **camp wagon**, team **(four mules or four oxen)**, cooking utensils and other necessaries of an outfit, he is ready to receive his purchases...and is then started out on the trail....'

This is another name for the trail boss.

These animals pulled the chuck wagon.

ON THE RANCH

As the trails grew more successful, Texas cattle farmers developed large ranches. These became busy communities where cowboys worked for much of the year.

At the heart of the ranch was the house where the owner's family lived. This was often a one-storey structure made of wood, or, in the south-west, adobe brick. It contained all the usual rooms of a family house, and an office, and was lit with candles or kerosene lamps. Cowboys slept in the bunkhouse. Some bunkhouses were barely furnished and men simply laid out their bedrolls on the floor. Others contained bunks and mattresses. Cowboys either cooked for themselves on the bunkhouse stove or ate in a special messhouse, where the ranch cook dished up food such as bacon and beans.

Cowboys carried out a variety of tasks on the ranch. Among the most important job was branding. This involved burning the owner's identifying mark, or brand, on to a cow's hide using a hot metal iron. Unbranded calves were known as mavericks, and were often stolen by rustlers as it was impossible to prove who owned them. Sometimes rustlers altered an existing brand using a running iron, a metal rod with no brand on the end that could be used to draw any shape.

Cowboys were also responsible for keeping cattle within the boundary, or line, of their ranch. Until a new ranch had fences, line riders patrolled the perimeter on horseback. They slept there, too, in a line camp. Once fences had been built, cowboys had to keep them in good repair.

Cowboys broke in untamed horses, known as broncos. This was not an easy task. A horse was caught using a lasso, blindfolded and saddled. Then a cowboy known as a bronco-buster sat on its back and pulled the blindfold off. At once the animal began to buck, while the cowboy tried to sit tight until it was exhausted. Then it could be tamed. Bronco-busters were often thrown from the saddle and sometimes broke limbs.

By the 1880s, the railroad had made the long cattle drives unnecessary. It also brought settlers, who built farms on the trails. As buffalo were driven from the northern plains (see pages 52-53), cattle were moved in and new ranches established. Many of these were funded by eastern businesses.

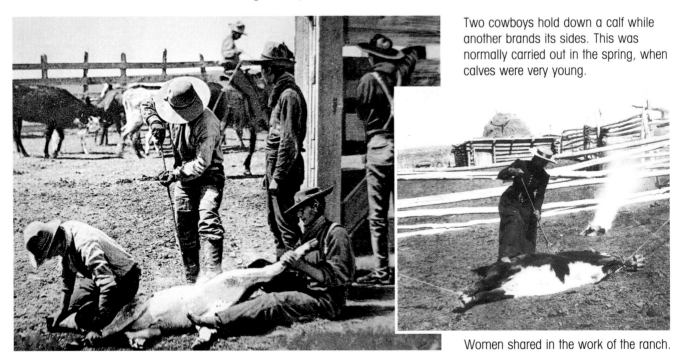

Two cowboys hold down a calf while another brands its sides. This was normally carried out in the spring, when calves were very young.

Women shared in the work of the ranch.

Texas cowboys. The ropes on the saddles, called lariats, or lassos, were used to catch cattle and horses.

COWBOY CLOTHES

Cowboys wore special clothes. Among these were chaps, leather leggings worn over trousers for protection, and cotton bandannas, which they tied around their mouths to keep out the dust. Their boots and hats were most distinctive. Cowboy boots were handmade from leather. They had high heels to stop the feet falling out of the stirrups, and thin soles for feeling the stirrups. Cowboy hats were usually made of felt. They had broad brims to keep off the sun, and high crowns so that air could circulate and cool the head. The most popular hat was the Stetson, made in Philadelphia.

In his memoirs, *We Pointed Them North* (1939), cowboy Teddy Blue Abbott tells this vivid story of an attempt to break a horse in that almost went tragically wrong. After the rescue, Bill (Charlton) offered Teddy a reward for saving his life. Teddy chose the horse that had caused all the trouble and kept it for the next 26 years.

The cantle is a raised section at the back of a saddle.

'... The horse cut up some and Bill got mad and **spurred** him. At that time they all had these Mexican spurs with long **rowels** and bells on them, and a long hook – a cinch hook it was called – on top of the rowell; ... Now Bill accidentally ran this hook into the **cinch ring**, and it caught there, and the horse bucked him off. He would have been kicked to death in a minute ... I got alongside Bill's horse and grabbed the cheek strap and threw myself out of the saddle. But my own spur caught on the **cantle**, and there I was stretched out for about a second between them two horses. Then I got loose and dropped to the ground, and got the cinches unbuckled and the saddle off and Bill out of it....'

Spurs are straps with spiked wheels attached to cowboys' boots. These were used to make a horse go faster.

A rowel is the wheel of a spur.

The cinch ring is attached to the cinch, a thick band buckled around a horse's body to keep the saddle on.

TOWN LIFE

Chinese, Mexicans and Europeans in a bar in San Francisco, California. The Chinese had to live apart and were allowed to do only certain jobs, such as laundry work or making clothes or cigars.

As settlers spread through the West, towns sprang up. Many grew up along trails and rivers – St Louis on the Mississippi, for example. Others began as mining towns. Virginia City, Nevada, owed its existence to the Comstock Lode (see pages 30-31). Cow towns such as Abilene formed around the railheads at the end of the cattle trails (see pages 36-37).

At first, most towns were little more than a wooden trading post, where goods could be bought, sold and exchanged. Gradually, other buildings formed a main street, which became the core of a community. A town generally followed a grid system, with the streets at right angles. Western towns were renowned for the width of their streets – a distance of 25m from side to side was not unusual. But in wet weather, these broad, unsurfaced roads became bogs, while in dry seasons they produced great clouds of dust.

General stores sold everything from sugar to guns, and saloons provided alcohol and entertainment. Hotels, banks (many producing their own notes and coins), sheriffs' offices, jails and courthouses were constructed, as well as schools and churches. When stagecoach and telegraph services developed (see pages 32-33), their offices opened. In some towns, there were libraries and theatres, and many communities produced a local newspaper.

San Francisco in 1850. This former Spanish mission grew into a busy sea-port. (See page 41.)

Frontier towns had much in common. The differences arose from the reason for a town's formation. Mining towns, for example, contained assay offices and often a segregated quarter where Chinese people had to live. In the early days, many cow towns were the scenes of violence, drunkenness and gambling. But as professionals and families moved in, most were tamed. Even in notorious Dodge City, guns were eventually banned. The nationality of a town's inhabitants also formed its character. St Louis, for example, was home to many German settlers, who maintained some of their European customs.

Not all frontier towns survived. Many mining towns, including Virginia City, became virtual ghost towns once the gold or silver was worked out. Cow towns faded with the disused trails. Other urban centres, such as Denver, adapted to changing conditions. Their success was often assisted by the arrival of the railroad (see pages 50-51), which provided a link with the raw materials and markets of the East.

In 1902, Owen Wister's novel, *The Virginian*, was published. Its author was a native of Philadelphia who in 1885 had spent some time in the cattle country of Wyoming. His book's central character, a cowboy known only as the Virginian, was a rugged but righteous hero. Wister helped to shape romantic ideas of the West that still persist, but he also captured some aspects of western life accurately. Here is his description of a frontier town.

'... until our language stretches itself and takes in a new word of closer fit, town will have to do for the name of such a place as Medicine Bow... [It had] twenty-nine buildings in all – one coal shute, one water tank, the station, one store, two eating-houses, one billiard hall, two tool-houses, one feed stable, and twelve others that for one reason and another I shall not name. Yet this wretched husk of squalor spent thought upon appearances; many houses in it wore a false front to seem as if they were two stories high.

Probably saloons and 'bawdy houses', where prostitutes lived and worked.

Between the 1840s and 1890s, San Francisco grew from 800 to 300,000 people. Thousands came by sea to search for gold, and trade opened up with the Far East. The *San Francisco Annals* of 1855 declared:

'... The San Franciscans are proud of their noble city that sits enthroned beside calm waters, and as Queen of the Pacific receives homage and tribute from all seas and oceans. ... The commerce of the Pacific is only beginning, ... Her spirit is GO AHEAD!... [from] a barren waste of sandhills – a paltry village – a thriving little town – a budding city of canvas, then of wood, and next a great metropolis of brick. In a few years more...she may be turned into ... Californian granite....'

COUNTRY LIFE

Prairie farms were often extremely isolated. Even if every plot had a family living on it, there was nearly a $\frac{1}{2}$ mile between them. Some families farmed larger plots, while speculators often owned substantial areas of land that remained empty until the selling price rose. Land was also set aside by the government for schools, and these plots, too, were not always used. As a result, many families lived between 1 and 2 miles from their nearest neighbour.

Country life revolved around the home. Usually, while men dealt with the heavy farm work, women's and children's work centred on the homestead, feeding animals or milking cows. Domestic work involved the preservation of fruit, vegetables and prepared meat to eat during the winter, when the ground was frozen and the town store – perhaps 90 miles away –

A country school, by Edward Lamson Herry, 1890. Most teachers were women.

beyond reach. The invention of the sewing machine in 1846 transformed clothes-making. The workload increased at certain times of the year, such as harvest, when helpers arrived from other farms and had to be fed.

Despite the difficulties, rural communities built social lives for themselves. In the summer,

children went to school and made friends there (schools often closed during the severe winters). Women gathered at each other's houses, sometimes to sew beautiful patchwork quilts during a 'quilting bee'. The occupants of several farms met for tasks such as raising barns. People organised fairs, too, with games, races and home-made food and drink for all to enjoy.

Religion also played its part in rural community-building. Churches were keen to establish congregations in the West. The government and railroad companies were glad to sell them land because they helped to bring order to the new territories. Clergy and their industrious wives often operated from buildings that were little more than shacks, or in the open air. But by organising services, Christmas and Easter

Gathering dried buffalo dung for fuel

celebrations and Sunday schools, they provided a focus for rural life. Many also set up hospitals, orphanages and other welfare institutions, as well as schools.

As time passed, improvements in transport and communications made contact between farms easier. Mail order catalogues and home delivery services brought the towns and the outside world within easier reach. By the end of the 19th century, rural isolation had greatly decreased.

Mail order catalogues made it possible for isolated farming families to buy all sorts of goods. This type of selling was begun in the USA in 1872 by Aaron Montgomery Ward.

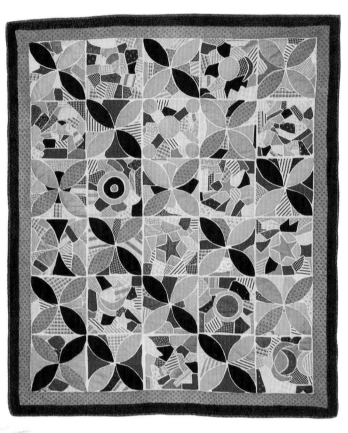

A 19th-century American quilt. Quilts were made with scraps of left-over material.

In 1872, Indiana farmer Uriah Oblinger bought a homestead on the prairies of Nebraska. In May the following year, his wife Mattie and baby daughter Ella joined him. Mattie wrote many letters to her mother about her experiences in the rural West.

'repairing' means 'preparing'.

People formed clubs and societies based on their hobbies and interests.

'Intemperance' here means drinking too much alcohol. Church-goers in particular believed that alcohol was evil, and formed Temperance Movements against it.

'January 11, 1880
... Uriah is repairing the minutes of the last Literary Society which was held last Saturday night. They have some big times debating. The question for next Saturday night is "Resolved that Intemperance causes more sorrow than war."... I go once in a while to hear them spout. We had rather a nice time...We had a Christmas tree at the schoolhouse. It was something new for this neighborhood. Everything went off nice and agreeable. We had a Norway spruce evergreen tree. It looked nice filled with presents for the little ones and some for the old ones. Uriah played Santa Claus but the little ones most all knew him...'

OUTLAWS AND VIOLENCE

The West attracted violent men – and women – because at first, law enforcement there was non-existent or ineffective. Western culture of the time also fostered violence. It was seen as praiseworthy to fight in defence of people or property. Revenge was regarded as justifiable, and physical courage was one of the highest ideals.

Gunfighters were among the most notorious outlaws of the West, and among the most feared was the Texan, John Wesley Hardin. Before he was 16, Hardin had killed four men. By the age of 42, when he was shot dead, the number had reached at least 20. New York-born orphan Billy the Kid was another sure shot, killing at least four men, including a sheriff, in the southwest. His varied crimes included petty theft and cattle-rustling.

Belle Starr 'Bandit Queen'. The story of her life as an outlaw was published (right).

Robber gangs who held up stagecoaches, banks and trains were another hazard of the West. The James Gang, headed by brothers Frank and Jesse James, was the first to carry out both a bank and a train robbery. They had been Confederate (southern) guerrillas in the Civil War, and Frank had taken part in the raid on Lawrence, Kansas (see pages 34-35). The gang showed no mercy as they carried out murderous raids. In their 15-year career, they attacked five stagecoaches, seven trains and 12 banks. Jesse James was eventually killed by a member of his own gang. Soon afterwards, Frank James surrendered and was pardoned.

The Wild Bunch, another violent gang, included the famous Butch Cassidy (real name George LeRoy Parker) and the Sundance Kid (Harry Longbaugh). Their hideout was the 'Hole in the Wall' in Wyoming, so they are sometimes known as the Hole in the Wall Gang, but this was a larger group of 100 or more outlaws, men and women, who all worked from the same base.

Horse- and cattle-thieving was a way of life for many Western criminals. Several famous rustlers were women, including Cattle Annie and her partner Little Britches, who operated in Oklahoma.

Outlaw Jesse James in his coffin

But the most formidable female bandit was the gun-toting Belle Starr, known as the Bandit Queen. Belle's father was a law-abiding farmer in Texas, but she rejected his middle-class lifestyle for a criminal career with Cherokee Blue Duck. Later she married another Cherokee, Sam Starr. Like Cattle Annie, Belle operated in Oklahoma. After a violent and eventful career, she was shot dead in 1889.

SOUTHWESTERN STRUGGLES

The southwest had its own brands of outlaws. The *Gorras Blancas* (White Caps), active in New Mexico during the 1890s, were Americans of Spanish descent. They resented the 'Anglos' – non-Hispanics and non-Native Americans – arrival on lands that they had farmed for many years. At night, wearing hoods and armed with guns, they cut fences, burned buildings and set loose animals. Similar conflicts occurred in California and Texas, where Hispanic *bandidos* (bandits) operated. Some were genuinely fighting Anglo intrusion. Others used this as an excuse for crime.

In 1881, the Governor of Missouri, Jesse James' home state, offered a reward of $25,000 for the outlaw's capture, dead or alive. He promised to pardon any member of the James Gang who gave evidence against his leader. Outlaw brothers Robert and Charles Ford accepted his offer. This account of James' death appeared in a newspaper in St Joseph, Missouri on 3 April 1882, where the killing took place.

REWARD

$15,000 REWARD FRANK JAMES DEAD or ALIVE

$5000 Reward for any Known Member of the James Band

$25,000 REWARD FOR JESSE JAMES

SIGNED

ST. LOUIS MIDLAND RAILROAD

'... Jesse said: "It's an awfully hot day." He pulled off his coat and vest and tossed them on the bed. Then he said, "I guess I'll take off my pistols for fear somebody will see them if I walk in the yard." He unbuckled the belt in which he carried two **45-caliber revolvers...** then picked up a dusting brush with the intention of dusting some pictures which hung on the wall ... His back was now turned to the brothers, who silently stepped between Jesse and his revolvers, ... both drew their guns. Robert was the quickest of the two ... Even in that motion, quick as thought, there was something that did not escape the acute ears of the hunted man. He made a motion as if to turn his head ... too late. A nervous pressure of the trigger, a quick flash, sharp report, and the well-directed ball CRASHED THROUGH THE OUTLAW'S SKULL. ...'

The calibre (American spelling 'caliber') of a gun is the diameter of the tube through which bullets travel.

LAW AND ORDER

Attempts to maintain law and order in the West took different forms. At first, ordinary citizens caught and punished criminals themselves. Then, as Western territories became states, officials began to enforce government laws.

In the early days, vigilantes, self-appointed guardians of law and order, banded together to track down criminals, who were punished without trial. Beating or tarring and feathering were common punishments, and criminals were also brought before 'Judge Lynch', or hanged (lynched). Vigilantism was open to abuse, since no one oversaw these activities. Many vigilante groups were run by the richest and most powerful people in a community, who pursued anyone who threatened their position or property.

The official law enforcement system had several levels. US marshals had state-wide responsibilities, while each town marshal had jurisdiction over a single community. Marshals were government appointed. They dealt with major crimes such as train robberies. Sheriffs, operating at county level, did not report directly to the government. They were locally elected, and dealt with small-scale crimes against citizens and property.

The distinction between law-enforcers and law-breakers was not always clear-cut. Wyatt Earp,

a skilled gunfighter with a chequered past, served as deputy marshal of Wichita and Dodge City, Kansas, then as US marshal of the Arizona Territory. In 1881, Wyatt, his three brothers and their friend Doc Holliday killed rustlers in a violent shoot-out at the OK Corral, Tombstone, Arizona. In films, this was made to represent the triumph of good over evil, but many historians now view it as a fight between two criminal gangs, one of which (the Earps) worked for wealthy ranch-owners.

Wild Bill Hickok was another two-sided character. An expert gunman, he became marshal in the cow town of Abilene, Kansas. His 'office' was a saloon, where he gambled at cards and drank. Always trigger-happy, he shot dead fellow-

A victim of 'Judge Lynch'. Murderer and robber John Heith was hanged in Tombstone Arizona, 22 February 1884.

Wyatt Earp, in about 1886

gambler Phil Coe in 1871. In 1876, he was himself killed during a poker game. Hickok's life was not, however, a stream of dramatic exploits. Like many other lawmen, including Wyatt Earp, his everyday duties included keeping the streets in good repair.

Government involvement in the West brought judges and juries to try and sentence criminals, as well as lawmen to capture them. Some judges were based in one town, while others, known as circuit judges, toured around. All played a vital part in curbing lawlessness.

This extract from *The Virginian* (see pages 40-41) describes the final encounter between the Virginian, an anti-rustler vigilante, and his arch-enemy Trampas. It inspired the main-street gun duels of many Westerns, and may itself have been inspired by a real incident involving Wild Bill Hickok.

'... The Virginian ... walked out into the open, watching. He saw men here and there, and they let him pass as before, without speaking. He ... gained a position soon where no one could come at him except from in front...

"It is quite a while after sunset," he heard himself say.

A wind seemed to blow his sleeve off his arm, and he replied to it, and saw Trampas pitch forward. He saw Trampas raise his arm and fall again, and lie there this time, still. A little smoke was rising from the pistol on the ground, and he looked at his own, and saw the smoke flowing upward out of it.

"I expect that's all," he said aloud. ...'

PRIVATE EYES

Allan Pinkerton was born in Glasgow in 1819. In 1842, he emigrated to Chicago, where he set up Pinkerton's National Detective Agency. In 1861, it uncovered a plot to assassinate President Abraham Lincoln, and during the Civil War, its detectives spied for the Union (northern) forces. In the West, the agency shadowed the Wild Bunch and the James Gang. The logo of the Pinkerton agency, an open eye with the slogan 'We Never Sleep', gave rise to the term 'private eye'.

The Pinkerton eye logo

BILLY THE KID

The legendary Billy the Kid was hunted down by Pat Garrett, the sheriff of Lincoln County, New Mexico. The young outlaw was sentenced to death, but escaped on 28 April 1881, the night before he was due to hang. Garrett pursued, cornered and killed Billy on 13 July that year. In 1882, the sheriff published *The Authentic Life of Billy, the Kid*, an inaccurate but fascinating biography of his victim.

THE ARMY

In the early 19th century, army officers such as Zebulon Pike (see pages 16-17) explored much Western territory. Then, in the fur-trading era, forts were established in the region to serve mainly as trading posts. In 1846, as many more settlers began to head west, the government agreed to build a network of forts for their protection, and soon the army had a widespread and permanent presence.

The role of soldiers in the West was wide-ranging. Their principal task was to protect migrants, miners, settlers and later railroad builders from Native American attack. Eventually, they were called upon to crush the Native Americans completely (see pages 52-53). In addition to military duties, the army built roads into the ever-expanding western territories and distributed supplies to reservations.

By the 1860s, there were about 100 army settlements in the West, from fully fledged forts to smaller garrisons or camps. Forts contained barracks, officers' quarters, stables and storehouses, and usually a central parade ground, where soldiers practised drills. A wooden stockade

A 'buffalo soldier' regiment, by Frederic Remington

or an adobe brick wall enclosed the fort. The wall around Fort Laramie, Wyoming, a former trading post that was bought by the government in 1849, was 40 ft wide and 20 ft high. Some smaller army posts were simply ramshackle groups of cabins.

After the Civil War (1861-65), many soldiers returned to the West, and more were recruited. Despite the poor conditions and low pay – about $13 dollars per month – recruitment was not difficult, as post-war unemployment was high. Some new recruits were criminals, while others were immigrants with no English, who had to watch other soldiers to find out what to do.

Fort Laramie by Alfred Jacob Miller, 1837, three years after it was built

About 15,000 soldiers served on the western frontier in the post-war era. In 1867, black troops – two regiments of infantry and two of cavalry – joined them for the first time. Native Americans called these men 'buffalo soldiers' because their hair reminded them of buffalo wool. Black soldiers had to endure a great deal of racism. Some whites, including General Custer (see pages 52-53), refused to work with them, while others demanded higher pay for doing so.

Fort life was harsh and dull. Soldiers froze in the glacial winters of the north and baked in the scorching summers of the southwest. They received severe punishments for even minor offences. If a soldier was judged to be dirty, for example, he had to carry a heavy log for 24 hours. Military diet usually consisted of bread or hardtack and poor-quality pork or beef. Disease, drunkenness and desertion were all commonplace.

Many soldiers objected to non-military duties such as building fort extensions. This soldier's complaint appeared in the *Army and Navy Journal* on 16 February 1867.

'... There has been no drills here the past winter, the soldiers being all occupied in building quarters. ... An officer cannot have proper discipline in his command under such circumstances ... desertions are more than frequent ... making dirt shovelers of soldiers may make them a source of profit in time of peace, but it is equally sure to make them worthless in time of war....'

THE TEXAS RANGERS

In 1823, Stephen F. Austin (see pages 22-23) set up a volunteer force to protect white Texans from Mexican and Native American attacks. Known as the Texas Rangers, the group became an official unit in 1835. The Rangers worked on horseback and were skilled gunmen and trackers. They still exist, based in the state capital, Austin.

In 1874, Captain Jack Summerhayes was sent to Arizona with his army unit. His wife, Martha, accompanied him and kept an account of the time she spent there:

The author is referring to the local Mexican women.

'camisa' is Spanish for 'blouse'.

'casa' is Spanish for 'house'.

'... The **women** were scrupulously clean and modest, and always wore, when in their **casa**, a low-necked and short-sleeved linen **camisa**, fitting neatly, with bands around neck and arms. Over this they wore a **calico** skirt; always white stockings and black slippers...

I have always been sorry I did not adopt their fashion of house apparel. Instead of that, I yielded to the prejudices of my conservative partner, and sweltered during the day in high-necked and long-sleeved white dresses, ate American food in so far as we could get it, and all at the expense of strength ...'

'calico' is unbleached cotton.

THE CHANGING WEST ACROSS THE CONTINENT

In 1862, after pressure from politicians and much disagreement about routes, the Pacific Railway Act was passed, authorising the building of a railroad across the centre of the USA. It also specified the substantial loans that the government would make to the railway companies for their work. These ranged from $16,000 to $48,000 dollars per mile, depending on the nature of the building land. The Act also laid down how much land along the route the government would grant to railroad companies. In 1864, a second Act was passed increasing both the loans and the land grants.

Two companies were chosen to construct the new track – the Central Pacific and Union Pacific Railroads. In 1863, laborers of the Central Pacific began to build east from Sacramento, California, as those of the Union Pacific began to build west from Omaha, on the Missouri River in Nebraska. The Central Pacific workers' task was the more difficult, as they had to blast a path through the Sierra Nevada mountains. Their leader, Charles Crocker, added 10,000 Chinese labourers to his team, to speed up progress. Often working in high winds and snowstorms, sometimes suspended over the rock face in baskets, they pushed doggedly onwards, although hundreds died.

In Nebraska, the Union Pacific leader General Grenville M. Dodge employed a 10,000-strong team, many of them ex-soldiers and recent Irish immigrants, to complete his 1,000 mile section of the railroad. (Crossing the mountains, Crocker and his men managed about 680 miles.) On 10 May 1869, the teams met at Promontory Point, Utah, and the last spike, made of gold, was driven in to complete the track. A telegraph message, 'Done', announced this great achievement to the world.

The first transcontinental railroad, and the four more that reached the Pacific coast by 1893, offered a quick, relatively safe way to travel to and from the West. At the same time, new rail routes within the West improved

Union Pacific labourers with their construction train in 1868. The train carried building materials for the new railroad.

transport across the region. The people and materials that the 'iron horse' imported and exported led to the development of flourishing new towns, farms and industries, and once more the region was transformed. But to the Native Americans of the Great Plains, the railroads brought only disaster (see pages 52-53).

In 1879, the Scottish writer Robert Louis Stevenson visited his fiancée Fanny Osbourne in the USA. He could afford only the most basic travel arrangements. In his book *Across the Plains*, he described his journey in an emigrant carriage of the Union Pacific Railroad.

'running from side to side'.

' ... an American railroad-car, that long, narrow wooden box, like a flat-roofed Noah's ark, with a stove and a convenience, one at either end, a passage down the middle, and **transverse** benches upon either hand. Those destined for emigrants on the Union Pacific are ... remarkable for their extreme plainness, nothing but wood ... and for the usual inefficacy of the lamps, which often went out and shed but a dying glimmer even while they burned. The benches are too short for anything but a young child....'

MONEY FOR NOTHING?
Government land grants and long-term loans (30 years) attracted 'get rich quick' speculators, who put down poor-quality tracks for immediate profit. Other, reputable, speculators constructed railroads through wilderness areas that might otherwise never have been settled. Only years later, when settlers had made the land productive and valuable, did these speculators profit.

The most famous railroad speculator of the era was New York investor Jay Gould (right). In the 1870s, he began to invest in western railroads. By 1890, he owned more than 12,000 miles of track, and the money he invested in the rail system brought both settlers and business to the West.

LAND OF OPPORTUNITY
Easier travel attracted thousands more immigrants. For example, between 1870 and 1914, about 12 percent of the population of Denmark emigrated to the USA.

NATIVE AMERICAN WARS

By the 1850s, it was clear that President Jackson's promise to the Native American peoples (see pages 20-21) had been empty. There were already many white settlers in the West beyond the Mississippi, and their numbers were growing. In September 1851, a meeting took place between government officials and about 10,000 of the Plains peoples at Fort Laramie in Wyoming. A treaty was signed in which each tribe agreed to live within a fixed territory and the government promised that these territories would remain Native American land forever.

The treaty soon crumbled. The new boundaries meant little to the Native Americans – they continued to hunt buffalo far and wide. Boundaries meant little to the white settlers, too, who went where they pleased. The situation worsened when railroad-building began. To clear the land of people and animals, professional hunters slaughtered the buffalo herds on which the Native American peoples depended. Soon government troops were in conflict with many different peoples who were trying to protect their lands and ways of life. Among the most important of these peoples was the Sioux.

Wars between the US army and the Sioux began in the 1850s. They intensified in the mid-1860s when miners opened a route called the Bozeman Trail through their hunting grounds. The Sioux, led by their chief, Red Cloud, attacked miners, settlers and three forts that the government was building on the trail. In December 1866, Sioux, Cheyenne and Arapaho warriors killed Captain William J Fetterman and about 80 soldiers.

To end the fighting, the government set up a Peace Commission. In 1868, in a second Fort Laramie treaty, it agreed to close the new forts, while the Native Americans promised to stop their attacks. To prevent further wars, the Commission decided that the peoples should live on special reservations. There they would be taught to farm and food would be provided. Some peoples reluctantly agreed to this policy. Others, including many Sioux, opposed it bitterly.

The final phase of the Sioux Wars began in 1874, when gold was discovered in the Black Hills of South Dakota. Soon miners began to flood into the area and violence flared again. At the Battle of The Little Bighorn on 25 June 1876, about 2000 warriors led by Chief Crazy Horse defeated some 250 soldiers under General George Armstrong Custer.

Soon, however, many Sioux were forced either to surrender or to go into exile in Canada. Others took comfort in a new ritual known as the Ghost Dance, which was intended to revitalise Native American culture. The army wanted to stamp out this new movement, and in 1890 massacred about 200 of its Sioux followers, at Wounded Knee, South Dakota. For the rest of the Sioux, reservation life was the only remaining option.

Custer's Last Stand, by Edgar Paxson, 1899. The artist shows the final stage of the battle of The Little Bighorn as more glorious than it really was.

Many young Native Americans were forced to attend European-style schools, dressed in European-style clothes.

THE DAWES ACT

In February 1887, the US government introduced a new law intended to destroy completely the Native Americans' way of life. The Dawes Act divided their homelands into plots of between 40 and 160 acres for farms. Those who agreed to live and work on these plots were granted American citizenship.

Chief Joseph

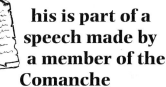 his is part of a speech made by a member of the Comanche people called Parra-Wa-Samen (Ten Bears). He speaks of his love for his homelands, and his misery at the prospect of reservation life.

A 'medicine lodge' is a low wood and buffalo hide hut in which a fire is built to produce steam. Native American men go inside to pray.

NAVAJO, APACHE AND NEZ PERCÉ

Native American peoples from throughout the West suffered similar fates to the Plains Sioux. In 1864, the US Army forced the Southwestern Navajo people to walk 300 miles – the Long Walk – to the reservation of Bosque Redondo, New Mexico. Drought killed the reservation crops and thousands of Native Americans starved. In 1868, the Navajo were allowed to return to a reservation in their homelands, where they flourished.

The Apache, also a Southwestern people, were living in reservations by 1873. But in 1882, and again in 1885, a group led by a man called Geronimo escaped. After leading resistance from Mexico, they surrendered in 1886.

Another tragedy unfolded on the High Plateau. The leader of the region's Nez Percé people, Chief Joseph, refused to take his followers to a reservation, but instead led them north towards Canada. However, the army forced them to surrender and moved them to a reservation in Kansas in 1877.

... You said that you wanted to put us on a reservation, to build us houses and make us medicine lodges. I do not want them. I was born on the prairie, where the wind blew free and there was nothing to break the light of the sun. I was born where there were no enclosures and where everything drew free breath. I want to die there and not within walls.

THE DECLINE OF THE COWBOY

Glidden's barbed wire advertisement, 1880. This invention transformed ranch life in the American West.

The construction of the railroads and the clearance of Native Americans and buffalo from the Plains brought four-and-a-half million people to the West between 1877 and 1887. Even the dry heart of the Great American Desert was settled by farmers from the USA, Europe and beyond.

About 6000 African Americans came from southern states such as Louisiana where, even after the abolition of slavery, they faced ill-treatment.

Unable to buy land, they worked as sharecroppers, paying the rent with a portion of what they grew, but payment terms were so harsh that they could not make a living. They were known as 'Exodusters', after the Bible story of the Exodus. Most Exodusters settled in Kansas and some in Oklahoma (see below).

Life was hard for the new Plains farmers (see pages 34-35), but improved farm machinery and new laws helped. Nature played its part, too. The

late 1870s and early 1880s were wet, making the land more fertile. Settlers thought that cultivating the soil changed the climate – 'Rain follows the plow' became a popular saying.

In the mid-1880s, the Plains suffered droughts, disproving theories of climate change. But the flow of immigrants was unstoppable. The government released 2 million acres of the Oklahoma District, the last fragment of Native American Territory, to settlement. There were extraordinary scenes on opening day, 22 April 1889. At the sound of a bugle, thousands of people charged forward on foot, on horseback or by any other means. In one day, 1.92 million acres were claimed in this astonishing land rush.

The new Plains farms ate into open grazing land traditionally

A land office, Kansas, where plots of land were allocated to settlers

used by cattle ranches (see pages 38-39), and the problem worsened after barbed wire was invented in 1874. This cheap, cattle-proof fencing material was popular with farmers and cattlemen alike, but as the ranges were more and more divided, fence-cutting wars broke out. In the terrible winters of 1886 and 1887, the wire proved fatal. As cattle stampeded out of the path of snowstorms, thousands of them piled into the fences and died.

Traditional ranching had been threatened following the 1881 invention of refrigerated wagons, making the transport of live cattle to market unnecessary. The losses of 1886 and 1887 effectively ended this in the north. Ranches grew smaller, and the cowboy's way of life was transformed for ever.

'Hard winter' by W.H.D. Koerner. Herding cattle on the northern ranges in winter was a terrible ordeal for cowboys.

SHEEP FARMING

As cattle-ranching on the northern plains declined, the importance of sheep grew. Competition between ranchers and sheep-owners for grazing land was intense. Cattlemen wanted sheep kept on dry, desert land where cows could not live successfully. So they often declared imaginary 'sheep deadlines', which they forbade shepherds to cross. Sometimes they even killed sheep. But their efforts were in vain. In Montana by 1900, there were about seven sheep for every cow.

In 1884, Theodore Roosevelt (later President) set up two ranches in Dakota Territory on the northern plains. He enjoyed ranch life and mourned its decline in his book, *The Wilderness Hunter* (1893):

'… No life can be pleasanter than life during the months of fall on a ranch in the northern cattle country. The weather is cool; in the evenings and on the rare rainy days we are glad to sit by the great fireplace, with its roaring cottonwood logs. But on most days not a cloud dims the serene splendor of the sky; and the fresh pure air is clear with the wonderful clearness of the high plains. We are in the saddle from morning to night.

'The best days of ranching are over … we who have felt the charm of the life … will not only regret its passing [for ourselves] but must also feel real sorrow that those who come after us are not to see, as we have seen, what is perhaps the pleasantest, healthiest, and most exciting phase of American existence….'

THE RISE OF INDUSTRY

Specially designed trains carry logs through Oregon, 1910

Industry as well as agriculture became a force shaping the West. The combination of a large population (20 million in 1900), new railroad links and abundant natural resources brought new forms of employment and economic success.

Mines in the Black Hills of South Dakota, where the discovery of gold prompted the final battles with the Sioux, were very profitable. Coeur d'Alene in Idaho produced large quantities of silver. By the 1880s, copper, increasingly used in electrical wiring, was a valuable commodity. It was mined first in Montana, then later in Utah and Arizona.

Wood from the cedar and fir trees of the Pacific Northwest had long been used locally as a building material and for mine construction. When the Northern Pacific Railroad reached

Portland, Oregon in 1883, timber could be transported and sold elsewhere. From about 1875 to 1900, timber was the most important industry in Texas. By

1900, the state had 637 sawmills, and the Kirby Lumber Company, valued at over $10 million, was its largest business. Texan lumber was transported out of the state by rail, and used within the state to extend the rail network.

In the early 20th century, the oil industry transformed life in Texas. Low-grade oil had been discovered in California and other western states in the 1860s, but the earliest important find in Texas took place in Corsicana in 1894. Companies and individuals were soon exploring other areas of the state. Many simply drilled into the ground anywhere and hoped for the best. This practice, which cost a great deal and often brought little reward, was generally known as wildcatting.

'Spindletop' Texas, 1901, the first 'black-gold' strike in the West

In 1901, the first huge strike of top-quality oil in the West occurred near the Texan town of Beaumont (see document). People hoping to make their fortune from 'black gold' poured in to the region. Companies such as Houston Oil sprang up, and by about 1910 the West was producing more oil than the older fields of John D. Rockefeller's Standard Oil in the East. For the cowboys, Texan oil success meant a further loss of ranch land.

Not all Western industries were based on natural resources. Factories produced a huge variety of goods, from farm machinery to steel pipes, and many country districts grew into towns. By the early 20th century, the Plains were home not only to farmers, but to dynamic and wealthy manufacturers and industrialists.

LOS ANGELES

In the 1880s, Los Angeles suddenly 'boomed', following the construction of new railroad links – with the Southern Pacific in 1876 and the Santa Fe in 1886. The competing railway companies advertised to attract customers and so prompted interest in the city. In 1900, Los Angeles had 102,000 inhabitants, but by 1930 almost 1.25 million people lived there. By then, the city was the centre of another successful western industry. Since 1911, studios in its Hollywood suburb had been making films.

A Hollywood Western film set in the 1920s

The Beaumont strike was made by drilling through a huge salt dome known as Spindletop. This is how the *Year Book for Texas*, 1901, described the dramatic event:

A 'derrick' is a structure that is built over an oil well and contains the drilling machinery.

'crude oil' is oil not yet refined into products such as gasoline and kerosene.

'… At exactly 10:30 a.m., the well that made Beaumont famous burst upon the astonished view of those engaged in boring it, with a volume of water, sand, rocks, gas and oil that sped upward with such tremendous force as to tear the crossbars of the derrick to pieces, and scattered … timbers, pieces of well casing, etc., for hundreds of feet in all directions.

For nine days the phenomenon was the wonder and puzzle of the world. It flowed unceasingly and with ever increasing force and volume until when it was finally controlled it was shooting upward a tower of pure crude oil, of the first quality, quite two hundred feet, and spouting in wanton waste 70,000 barrels of oil per day....'

Conclusion

In 1850, American publisher and politician Horace Greeley issued his famous appeal: 'Go West, young man, and grow up with the country.' Throughout the 19th century, thousands of Americans, women, men and children, did make the journey from east to west across their continent (see document). Then, with perseverance and courage, they carved out new lives in what was for them a new land.

But the story of the American West is not that of the farming pioneers alone. It is also the story of the early fur-traders, the get-rich-quick prospectors, the free-roaming cowboys, railroad-builders, shop-keepers, homesteaders and numerous others, many of whom arrived by different routes from different countries. This extraordinary mixture of people, and the huge variety of motives that drove them, combine to make the tale of this vast region compelling.

These migrants did not settle on uninhabited ground. They arrived in a land that had for thousands of years been home to Native American peoples. To them, much of the West was not only beautiful but sacred, the place where their gods and goddesses lived and their ancestors were buried. So what the newcomers experienced as gain – the acquisition of land – the Native Americans experienced as loss, of their territory, their livelihood and their freedom.

In 1883, former buffalo hunter Buffalo Bill (real name William Cody) set up a Wild West show. Its members, including Chief Sitting Bull, acted out events of Western history, from the Battle of The Little Bighorn to stagecoach robberies. But the drama was more exciting than realistic.

The history of the American West is so dramatic that it has inspired countless writers and film-makers. But many of them have represented it in an unrealistic way. For example, though there were large numbers of black cowboys, and Chinese workers, few are ever seen in films. Likewise, though few overlanders were killed by Native Americans, such murders were commonly portrayed in Westerns. It is important to disentangle the reality of the West from the myths that have grown up around it so that the remarkable truth is remembered.

Today, the West continues to attract settlers from all around the world, and its unique history continues to unfold.

This painting of Piekan people by George Catlin shows a vanished way of life.

Migrants never forgot their time on the overland trail. Although there were great hardships, there was also friendship and generosity of a kind not often experienced in more settled communities. This entry from the *Gold Rush Diary* of Elisha Perkins, dated 11 July 1849, explains this more fully.

'... We were told great stories about the selfishness & want of feeling among the Emigrants ... [yet] Never have I seen so much hospitality and good feeling ... as since I have been on this route. Let any stranger visit a camp no matter who or where, & the best of everything is brought out .... If at meal time the best pieces are put on his plate & if the train has any luxuries they are placed before him. Nor have I seen any man in trouble, deserted, without all the assistance they could render. ...'

Sioux chief Red Cloud summed up his experience of white settlement in the West. While to many white Americans the frontier seemed to be expanding, to the Native Americans it seemed to be shrinking, until only the reservations were left.

... They made us many promises, more than I can remember, but they never kept but one; they promised to take our land, and they took it...'

NATIVE AMERICAN RESERVATIONS

By the 1890s, Native Americans were confined to reservations, shown in orange on this map.

This extract from the US Bureau of the Census report for 1892 proclaims the end of the frontier. It marks the 'official' end of the West.

'... Up to and including 1880 the country had a frontier of settlement, but at present the unsettled area has been so broken into by isolated bodies of settlement that there can hardly be said to be a frontier line. In the discussion of its extent and its westward movement it can not, therefore, any longer have a place in the census reports...'

GLOSSARY

adobe brick made from sun-dried mud.

assay test for the purity of gold or silver.

Aztec a civilisation that flourished in Mexico from the 14th century AD. It was conquered by the Spanish during the years from 1519 to 1521.

bandanna a square of material that a cowboy folded into a triangle and wore around his neck or over his nose and mouth to keep out dust.

blasphemous offensive to God.

brand a mark burned into a calf's skin with a hot iron as a sign of ownership.

buckskin the skin of a buck (male) deer.

buffalo American bison, dark-coloured cattle with huge heads and humped backs.

chuck wagon a wagon that carried food (chuck) and other supplies on cattle drives. It was also where the food was cooked.

Conestoga wagon a long, heavy wagon made in Conestoga Valley, Pennsylvania.

conquistador a Spanish word meaning 'conqueror'. It is used to describe the Spanish invaders who colonised lands in the Americas during the 16th century.

culture area one of ten areas in North America whose Native American peoples developed similar lifestyles.

empresario a coloniser of Texas when it was under Mexican rule (1821-36).

Exodus the Israelites' flight from Egypt, where they were held as slaves. The story appears in the book of Exodus in the Bible.

hardtack hard, square biscuits made from wheat.

hickory any of several North American trees that bear edible nuts and have very tough wood.

hunter-gatherer a person hunts animals and gathers plants for food.

Ice Age any period when much of the Earth was covered with ice. The last Ice Age began about 1.6 million years ago and ended about 11,000 years ago.

Inca a civilisation that flourished in Peru from the early 12th century. It was conquered by the Spanish in the 1530s.

linsey-woolsey a coarse material made of linen and wool.

lodge (beaver) a dome-shaped shelter built over a river and made of wood, stones and mud.

lodge (Native American) a large family dwelling, usually made of reeds and grasses or mud.

maverick an unbranded calf.

Midwest a large area of the north central USA. It includes Illinois, Iowa, Wisconsin, Minnesota, Nebraska, Kansas, Missouri and the Dakotas. Also those portions of Montana, Wyoming and Colorado east of the Rocky Mountains. Ohio, Michigan and Indiana are often included.

militia an army of private citizens rather than professional soldiers.

mission a church and other buildings from where missionaries work to convert Native Americans to Christianity.

Morse Code an international telegraph code in which each letter and number is represented by a different combination of dots and dashes.

mountain man a fur-trapper, guide or other adventurer who lived in and explored the Rocky Mountains from about 1810 to 1840.

New Spain territories outside Spain that were ruled by the Spanish from the 16th to the 19th century. They consisted of the American Southwest, Mexico, parts of Central America and the

West Indies and the Philippine islands of South-East Asia.

New World North, South and Central America, whose lands were 'new' to the European explorers of the 15th and later centuries. The part of the world that Europeans knew before they arrived in the Americas is called the Old World.

overlander a person on the overland trail to the American West.

pit-house a house built wholly or partly below ground.

polygamy marriage to several wives at the same time.

prairie schooner a smaller version of the Conestoga wagon (see above). They looked like ships (schooners) sailing across the grass 'sea' of the prairies.

presidio a Spanish fort.

Pueblo a Spanish word meaning 'village' and used to describe village-dwelling Native American peoples of the Southwest.

range a large area of uncultivated, open land used for grazing cattle.

redwood a type of huge, cone-bearing tree that grows along the Californian coast. Redwoods can reach a height of 300 ft.

reservation an area of land set aside (reserved) for Native Americans evicted from their own territories. Reservations were often established on infertile land that was almost impossible to farm, and many people starved.

Rio Grande a river that flows south from the Rocky Mountains in Colorado to the Gulf of Mexico. Much of its length forms the border between Mexico and the USA. In Mexico it is called the Rio Bravo.

rustler a cattle thief.

salt dome layers of rock in a dome shape around a salt core. Salt domes often trap oil rising from deep under the ground.

Sierra Nevada a mountain range in eastern California.

sod house a house made from pieces of turf (sod). It was also known as a 'soddy'.

speculator a person who buys land or property to sell for profit.

stockade a fence made of large stakes or planks of wood.

Texas longhorns wild, hardy Texas cattle descended from the cows kept on Mexico's Spanish missions.

tipi a tent-like structure made of buffalo hides stretched over a wooden framework.

totem pole a wooden pole carved with animal symbols representing a Native American clan or family (from the Pacific Northwest culture area).

wagon train a group of wagons that journeyed overland to the West. Some trains were made up of just a few wagons, others contained 150 or more.

INDEX